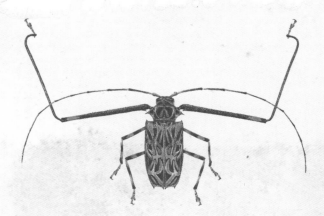

THE
BEETLE
COLLECTOR'S
HANDBOOK

As featured in the bestselling Beetle Boy books!

M.G. LEONARD

FEATURING ILLUSTRATIONS BY
CARIM NAHABOO

SCHOLASTIC

FOR THE YOUNG AT HEART, CURIOUS, QUESTIONING AND BRAVE.

Scholastic Children's Books
An imprint of Scholastic Ltd
Euston House, 24 Eversholt Street, London, NW1 1DB, UK
Registered office: Westfield Road, Southam, Warwickshire,
CV47 0RA
SCHOLASTIC and associated logos are trademarks and/or
registered trademarks of Scholastic Inc.

First published in the UK by Scholastic Ltd, 2018

Text copyright © M.G. Leonard Ltd, 2018
Beetle illustrations copyright © Carim Nahaboo, 2018

The right of M.G. Leonard to be identified as the author of this
work has been asserted by her.

ISBN 978 1407 18566 8

Printed in Malaysia

This is a work of fiction. Names, characters, places, incidents
and dialogues are products of the author's imagination or are used
fictitiously. Any resemblance to actual people, living or dead,
events or locales is entirely coincidental.

www.scholastic.co.uk

Baxter!
see page 38

CONTENTS

Marvin is
the
BEST!
p. 92
V.C.W.

Lucretia
Cutter
page 32!
Her spies
page 118
Her
soldiers
page 78

NEWTON!
p. 63

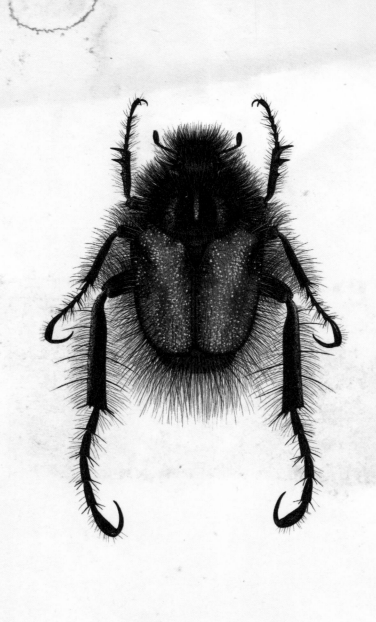

INTRODUCTION

By way of introduction, allow me to tell you that my name is Dr Montgomery George Leonard, and I am a <u>coleopterist.</u> I study those charismatic six-legged beasties we call beetles. That may sound terribly grand, and I'll admit that I proudly puff out my chest when I'm at the Savile Club and people ask about my chosen career, but the truth is anyone can do it. The qualifications you need to be a coleopterist are as follows: you must be young at heart, curious, questioning and brave, and I feel I must be frank about this, you must also be able to cope with the stomach-curdling smell of animal droppings, for there are many scarabs who love nothing more than a fresh mound of dung.

I have filled the pages of this book with six-legged

creatures to dazzle and amaze you. Once you have read it, you will want to thrust the book before the tired eyes of your grown-ups, saying 'Look!' and 'Did you know...?' They will be impressed, of course; how could they not be? It is then, that you must ask, nay demand, to be taken to the wilds of your nearest green habitat, to discover what insect friends might be living there.

When you set out on expeditions of discovery, be sure to take this book with you. It is stuffed with helpful information about being an entomologist (a studier of insects), and luckily it is the kind of book that increases in value the more grass stains and mud smears it accumulates.

It was on my first expedition to Ecuador – as a zoology student with a thesis to write on the feeding habits of the spider monkey – that I first fell in love with Coleoptera. For what is there not to love about beetles? Whether they're firing boiling acid from their bottoms, letting rip a foul stinking death fart, rolling dung or navigating by the Milky Way, there's no end of things to delight in when studying beetles. They are warriors, speedsters and clowns. In short, dear reader, it is impossible to be bored when one has a relationship with beetles.

It was apparently an observation first made by the British scientist Mr J. B. S. Haldane that the Creator

bombard beetles?

death fart!
Heh! Heh!

6

must have 'an inordinate fondness for beetles' for their species are as numerous and countless as the stars. This fondness is something I often think about as I lie on my back in the grass staring up at the night sky*, for the beetle is the single most successful creature on the planet. You may think this planet belongs to us, but I hope you won't be alarmed when I inform you that actually, it belongs to the beetles.

After considerable thought I have made some decisions about the content of this, *The Beetle Collector's Handbook*.

Firstly, I have selected the species of beetle that I think are the most surprising, beautiful and impressive, in the hope this will inspire further reading and exploration.

Secondly, there are many ways to arrange the contents of a book, and I have decided to shun the traditional, taxonomy-based listing of species, which is rather like a dictionary and only helpful if you know what you are looking for. Instead I have chosen a more playful grouping of beetles by shared traits, skills or appearance. I appreciate this approach is hardly scientific, and there will be many of my esteemed colleagues at the <u>Royal Entomological Society</u> who will shake their heads and tut, but my intention is not to be comprehensive; rather,

How old do you have to be to become a member? Is there a test?

---

* If you have never done this, then you must, immediately. Allow me to recommend the habit to you at least once every summer.

to cause you to marvel and become excited.

Thirdly, there is a scientific language that is commonly used when describing insects, and much of it is in Latin. I was not a strong Latin scholar at school and understanding the words seems alien. Nonetheless, some Latin words are too important to be done away with. So I have kept my language plain and only used a scientific word where none else will do.

You see, young entomologist, you are very important, and I don't want the number of beetles to overwhelm you, or old-fashioned language to put you off. You have a vital role to play in protecting this planet. Whether you are exploring a rainforest or your own garden or a park, you are learning how our ecosystem works. This knowledge will bring you great joy and wonder, and I hope a desire to share your findings with others. My motto throughout this book is that we should observe, respect and protect the wildlife we have, for it is disappearing at an alarming rate.

It has not escaped my attention that my generation of entomologists have almost exclusively been wealthy gentlemen. There have been important women in the history of entomology, none more so than Maria Sibylla Merian, a German artist who was one of the very first to draw insects alive in their natural habitats. She

Must learn Latin

Latin = secret code

I swea to protec nature D.A.C.

Find out about Maria Merian.

8

published *Metamorphosis of the Insects of Surinam* in 1699. As the human race continues to spread across the green surface of the Earth, transforming it into bricks and mortar, it is vital that all girls and boys understand and admire beetles and other invertebrates. So, I would like to make it clear that this book is most definitely for girls. There can be no gender bias when it comes to protecting the wildlife of this planet. Bugs are for girls, boys and everyone with a passion for conservation.

Yaaasss! V.C.W.

I'm at the end of my adventuring days now. As I sit in my leather-backed armchair, I dream of one last expedition to Ecuador, but my knees are those of an arthritic old man and refuse to carry me anywhere that doesn't serve tea at three o' clock with a scone, some clotted cream and homemade raspberry jam. Unable to venture forth, I have decided to dedicate my time to writing books about beetles. This is my first, and I do hope you find it useful.

Yours faithfully,

VIRGINIA, KEEP OUT!!!
of my book
D.A.C.

Monty G. Leonard

PREPARING FOR AN EXPEDITION

The most thrilling and delightful moments of my life have occurred when I've been on an expedition. You cannot predict what you will see, or adventures you're going to have, out in the wild with nothing but wit and wisdom to guide you. I always learn something on an excursion, even if I'm not far from home. I remember learning, at the age of eight, that one should always wear long trousers, and not short, when on a bug hunt. This is in case you walk along a fallen tree trunk and are misfortunate enough to lose your balance and fall into a sea of nettles. This was a painful lesson, and not one I'm likely to ever forget.

Before you head out on a beetle-hunting expedition, you will need to arm yourself with knowledge and select the right tools, and long trousers, for the job. Do you know what you are looking for? Where will you find it, and when should you search for it?

For example, if you are hoping to see a stag beetle in Britain there are only a few months of the year when you might spot the adult – between the end of March and June. It lays its eggs near rotting wood – because that is what the larvae feed upon – so you are most likely to spot your quarry in a place where there is plenty of decaying timber, like a forest.

Unless they live on Beetle Mountain

Often there is a time of day or night when a beetle will be out and about. For example, a chafer, or May bug, flies at dusk. Learning this kind of information will ensure your expeditions are successful.

You can find beetles in almost every habitat on earth, from ponds to deserts, with the exception of the frozen wastes of the Arctic and Antarctic, or salt seawater. They come in all shapes and sizes, so how will you know when you've seen one?

WHAT IS A BEETLE?

A beetle is an insect with two distinguishing characteristics. The beetle's sheathed wings are its most recognisable feature. The hard forewings are called elytra, and they protect the more delicate hindwings folded beneath. When the beetle is on the ground, the elytra are held against the abdomen, usually meeting in a straight line down the middle of the beetle's back. When it is in flight, the elytra are held out for balance and the membranous hindwings do the flying. Coleoptera means 'sheath wings', and is the name of the scientific order for beetles.

The other distinguishing characteristic (in combination with elytra) is that beetles have mouthparts, made for chewing, called mandibles. Different species of beetle prefer different meals, ranging from wood, plants, manure, rotting matter, fallen fruit, and even other invertebrates, so their mandibles differ. However, despite not closing their mouths when they are eating, they all chew their food thoroughly before swallowing.

The beetle body has an exoskeleton and three main sections: the head, the thorax and the abdomen. This last section is further divided into segments or rings, like

BANANAS!

12

a suit of armour, so it can bend. The wings and legs are attached to the thorax and not to the abdomen. A beetle's head has compound eyes (eyes made of many lenses), antennae (sometimes called feelers) and mandibles. The antennae are used to smell and taste the air and detect the pheromones of female beetles. Beetles breathe through tiny holes, called spiracles, along the sides of their bodies.

Beetles vary dramatically in size from the microscopic featherwing beetle (measuring less than a millimetre in length) to the gigantic Titan (measuring twenty centimetres). Coleoptera is not a 'one size fits all' order, and though the big beetles are impressive, the smaller ones can be just as fierce.

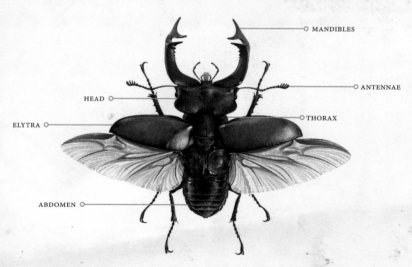

MANDIBLES

ANTENNAE

HEAD

THORAX

ELYTRA

ABDOMEN

FIG. 1. LUCANUS CERVUS (STAG BEETLE)

LIFE CYCLE

I t's important to note that beetles don't always look like … *beetles*. You may be surprised to learn that during a beetle's life it will pass through four stages of development: egg, larva, pupa and imago (adult). This life cycle is called a complete metamorphosis, meaning change of form. The length of each of these four different stages varies depending on the species.

The beetle begins life as an egg. A beetle's egg is somewhat smaller than the type you may have fried or boiled for breakfast. It is more like the size of caviar, which are fish eggs that are delicious on a thin piece of toast. From the beetle's egg emerges a larva; this is the second stage and the only growing period for the beetle. Some larvae grow quickly, while others are slow, and most of them change their skins several times as they grow. Each period within one skin is called an instar. When the larva has eaten enough to make the big change, it enters the third stage and becomes a pupa. It hides away and lies still as it goes through a physical transformation, changing from larva to imago. This period can last anything from a day up to a year or so, depending on the species.

From the pupa emerges an adult beetle. This is the fourth and final stage, and the most visible creature for beetle collectors, as it usually lives above ground. At first the beetle's body will be limp and damp, its wings unfit for flying. The beetle needs time to complete the change and harden its exoskeleton. The adult beetle may eat, but it will never grow.

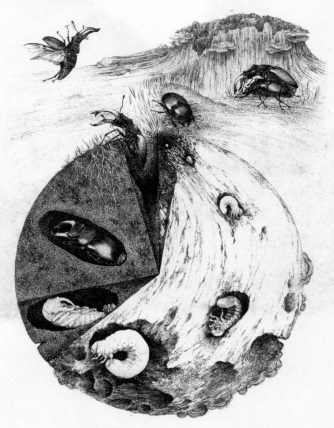

FIG. 2. THE LIFE CYCLE OF A STAG BEETLE

WHAT'S IN A NAME?

To describe all of the living things on the planet is an enormous and complex job. A long time ago some clever chaps in Ancient Greece decided we should arrange living things into groups that share characteristics. Many hundreds of years later Carl Linnaeus, a Swedish botanist, invented a naming system that became the foundation of biological classification today, hence the name Linnaean taxonomy. Carl Linnaeus must have been a tremendously clever chap, because I have a naming system for my grandchildren – who number fewer than twenty – and I still muddle them up at Christmas.

The naming system for living things divides them into KINGDOMS: the animal kingdom and the plant kingdom, for example. Then each of these kingdoms is divided into groups called PHYLA, then each phylum is divided into groups called CLASSES, classes are divided into ORDERS, orders into FAMILIES, families into GENERA and finally each genus into SPECIES. This may seem complicated, but think about how many living things there are on this planet, and how different you are from a beetle, and yet you both need to be classified within the same system!

Every scientist on the planet follows the rules of the Linnaean taxonomic system and uses the language chosen for the naming system, which is Latin. Thus we ascribe a unique scientific Latin name to each and every living thing, and this name carries valuable information; it's like a secret language for those of us in the Latinate know, *Scientia potentia est.*

Now, a scientific name is different from a common name. For example you may say you have a pet hamster called Terrence, whereas a scientist would say you have a pet *Mesocricetus auratus* called Terrence. If a scientist were to give Terrence his full classification they could say:

BAXTER=

KINGDOM:	Animalia,	Animalia
PHYLUM:	Chordata,	Arthropoda
CLASS:	Mammalia,	Insecta
ORDER:	Rodentia,	Coleoptera
FAMILY:	Cricetidae,	Scarabaeidae
GENUS:	*Mesocricetus,*	Chalcosoma
SPECIES:	*auratus.*	caucasus

Which is a grand way of describing Terrence as an animal with a spine, a small mammal, a rodent distantly related to voles and lemmings, which we recognise as a hamster, specifically the golden hamster.

Now that you've absorbed all that, you may put it out of your mind. We will never mention Terrence again. All you need to know is that there is a system for naming things, and it's going to help you identify and understand the beetles you find on your expeditions.

BEETLE CLASSIFICATION

Brace yourself for an astounding fact: beetles make up nearly a quarter of all the known living species on Earth. There are between 360,000 and 400,000 described species of beetle in collections around the world, and probably at least another million beetles out there waiting to be discovered. This is an incredible number when you compare it to the ten thousand species of birds and five thousand species of mammals on this planet. This is why entomology is such fun. There are always discoveries to be made, and these marvellous creatures help us develop a deeper understanding of the natural world. With there being so many beetles, understanding the organisation system for them can be a little confusing, but all you have to remember is that the beetles are put into groups that share the same physical characteristics. If two beetles look alike they are probably from the same family.

There are four suborders of Coleoptera, but only two to which nearly all families of beetles belong. These are Adephaga, which includes ground beetles and aquatic beetles, and Polyphaga, which contains nearly ninety per cent of all beetle species, including scarabs,

Titchy number

YES!

fireflies, ladybirds and darkling beetles.

In this handbook I have stuck to common names and noted the family the beetle comes from, using scientific names when I need to make it clear which beetle I'm describing.

~

AN ENTOMOLOGIST'S BACKPACK

Before you set out on an expedition, you'll want to be sure you've got all the essential equipment you might need. Over time you'll develop your own kit, but here are what I believe to be the entomologist's essentials:

Marmite & salt and vinegar crisp sandwiches + juice

- Cucumber sandwiches, potted shrimp and a flask of tea.
- You will also need a notebook and pencil for writing down the species of beetle you spot on your expedition. You will want to record the date, time, habitat, species name and describe its behaviour.
- Drawing what you see in your notebook will help

19

you study the beetle closely, so bring coloured pencils.

- A field guide is handy to help you identify the creatures you collect.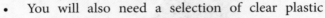

- Every entomologist worth their salt has a pooter in their pocket (see opposite page for instructions), to suck up an insect for closer inspection.

Or a giant pooter backpack! :)

- You will also need a selection of clear plastic tubs and pots for storing insects, to allow you to take a closer look. These needn't be fancy: small tupperware or recycled kitchen containers will do, as long as the lids let air in and they are thoroughly washed.

- A sweep net (see page 22), which can be made from an old tennis racket, is good for collecting insects on plants. A butterfly net is perfect for capturing flying beetles. If you are fishing for aquatic beetles, you'll need a pond net.

- A beating tray (see page 22) will help you collect insects falling from shaken tree branches.

- And if you are looking for nocturnal beetles you will need to set up an insect light trap, which can be as simple as hanging a white sheet on your washing line and shining a torch at it.

- If you are lucky enough to have one, I suggest you bring a camera, although it is not essential.
- You will need a magnifying glass or hand lens for close examination, and if possible you should get a stereo microscope to have at home.

None of this equipment need be expensive and most of it you can make yourself.

MAKE YOUR OWN POOTER

A pooter, sometimes called an aspirator, is used to catch small insects. It is like a tiny vacuum cleaner. You suck in through one tube, which is connected to a holding chamber, and hold the second tube – the vacuum nozzle – close to the beetle you wish to collect. When you breathe in, the beetle is sucked up the tube into the chamber. A gauze across the end of the breathing tube ensures you never accidentally swallow the beetle.

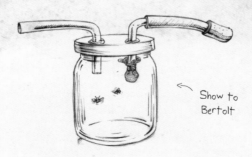

Show to Bertolt

A sweep net is a tough net with a canvas bag rather than netting. You use it to collect insects from plants and long grass by swinging it from side to side as you walk through a field or down a hedgerow. The rim and canvas must be robust to withstand the impact of jarring against plants, and so a butterfly net will not do. I have found it is simple enough to make one's own sweeping net with an old tennis racket and a pillowcase.

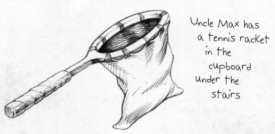

Uncle Max has a tennis racket in the cupboard under the stairs

MAKE YOUR OWN BEATING TRAY

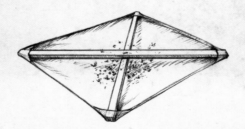

A beating tray is held beneath the branches of a tree, which you give a sharp tap with a stick so that insects on the leaves or branches fall on to the tray. You can

then collect the beetles with your pooter, to examine and document them. Making a beating tray can be as simple as stretching a white piece of cloth over an old kite frame.

BEFRIENDING BEETLES

It isn't necessary for a collector to venture far out into the wild to find beetles to study. If you are lucky enough to have a garden, why not bring the beetles to you?

Here are a few things you can do to help our insect friends and bring beetles to your back door.

BUILD A LOG PILE   or a mountain of teacups!

Some people's hearts lift at the sight and scent of a beautifully arranged bouquet of flowers, but I delight in a pile of logs, sticks and dead leaves. My neighbours often make rude comments about my garden being an overgrown tangle of ivy and buddleia. They make loud remarks about the decaying logs and dead seed heads that stand, poker-like, in the tall grass. But my garden is the perfect place for a bug hunt and I would not change a thing.

Log piles are a great addition to any garden because the damp and rotting wood creates a perfect habitat in which female beetles of many species can lay their eggs, and it also provides food for the larvae.

If you build a log pile it won't just benefit beetles. Other creatures, such as bees, spiders, woodlice, centipedes, slugs, toads and even hedgehogs, may move in.

How to make log piles:

1. Choose various locations in your garden, both cool and warm.
2. Gather logs of various sizes, twigs, sticks, bark and dead leaves.
3. Dig down fifty centimetres and plant some logs vertically, sticking up out of the ground, and fill in the hole with soil. Then add leaves and bark.
4. Lay other logs higgledy-piggledy across and around the vertical logs and stuff holes with twigs, sticks and dead leaves.
5. Leave the piles to rot, adding new logs each summer.
6. If you are worried about the piles looking unsightly, plant creepers to grow across them. This will also help to keep moisture in.

In a short time you will spot lots of beetles in your own garden.

or a beetle suitcase

You don't need a big garden with log piles to bring beetles to your home; why not open a bug hotel? A bug hotel can be as small as a bird box, hung on an exterior wall in a sunny, south-facing spot. Or if you have a garden you can build a bug hotel as big as a beehive.

How to make a bug hotel:

1. Choose a spot for your bug hotel where the ground is level. WARNING! Don't build it beside your vegetable garden, otherwise the insects will assume your greens are their room-service and eat them all up!

2. Build the foundations using strong materials such as bricks or wooden pallets. Then layer on other smaller building materials like dead wood, bamboo canes, reeds or bits of terracotta plant pot.

3. Collect and then stuff the gaps with dry leaves, straw and corrugated cardboard.

4. Once you've built up several layers of natural materials, add a roof. You can make this with old planks, bits of slate or roof tiles.

5. Decorate your hotel with a magnificent sign and plant some wildflower seeds around it to attract the most stylish residents.

The single greatest joy of being a beetle collector comes
 from observing beetles in their natural habitat, seeing them
fly, or feed, or mate. As a beetle collector it is important you
have a notebook to write down and draw all of the beetles
you find. With a camera, you can photograph the beetle

need!!

close up for anatomical detail, and in its natural habitat,
and add these images to your notebook. Drawing a beetle
is a very good way of noticing everything about it, and I
find it helps me remember it clearly.

YOUR FIELD JOURNAL

All you need to create your own field journal is a
notebook the size of an exercise book, preferably with
blank pages. Mine is like a diary. Before I set out on an
expedition, I write the date and a sentence or two about
where I'm going to be spending my day and what the
weather is like. Then I have a system of writing things
down that I repeat for each beetle I find.

I lay out my field journal thus...

*I'm going to do this for all
the beetles in the mountain.*

DATE:	*Wednesday the 16th of July, 1902*

*Today I will be visiting Richmond Park. The weather is
uncomfortably warm, and requires an open collared, short-sleeved
cotton shirt. True to English form, it rained heavily yesterday,
but I'm hoping the soft ground will bring forth the beetles.*

BEETLE:	*Ladybird*	FAMILY:	*Coccinellidae*
NAME:	*Coccinella septempunctata*	PICTURE:	
TIME:	*11:45 am*		
LOCATION:	*Isabella Plantation in Richmond Park*		
HABITAT:	*Red rose bush*		
STAGE:	*Imago – adult*		
NUMBER:	*One beetle*		

WHAT DOES IT EAT: *Greenfly*

WHAT EATS IT: *Spiders*

NOTES:

*It was eating greenfly. It has one leg missing. It has seven spots.
It is scarlet red with black spots.*

RECORDING YOUR FINDINGS

There may be discoveries you make, whilst beetle hunting, that require you to report your findings. For example, the stag beetle population in England is declining, so if you see one and note down its particulars you can be part of a national recording project that maps the species and its population. If you identify a beetle as being alive that was previously thought to be extinct, or discover a beetle that doesn't appear to have been described before, your local natural history museum or university department is the perfect place to take such a discovery.

You can record your regular wildlife findings in official recording schemes. The information that you have collected will benefit working scientists. By providing them with important biodiversity information you will be contributing to nature conservation, research and education. Both the Amateur Entomologists' Society and the Royal Entomological Society will be able to provide you with details of recording schemes.

BODY SNATCHING

One of the handy things about beetles is that they are invertebrates with exoskeletons, so if you keep your eyes open you will find dead dung beetles, stags and chafers at the times of year when adults have mated and died naturally. These you can pick up, take home and collect, although I should warn you, dead beetles are a bit pongy.

THE BEETLES

A tasting menu of the most intriguing, shocking, adorable and downright unbelievable beetles on the planet.

COLOSSAL COLEOPTERA

G iant insects are considered to be the stuff of nightmares. However, when it comes to gigantic beetles, you will find that these clumsy herbivores are more likely to charm than horrify.

Charles Darwin suggested that to realise the true majesty of a beetle, we should imagine it to be the size of a dog or a horse. The colossal Coleoptera described here are merely the size of a house sparrow or a bat, but they are impressive nonetheless, especially when they fly.

A question I am frequently asked is, which beetle is the biggest? This line of enquiry leads to a spirited debate.

The heavyweight title is currently held by the larval stage of the Goliath beetle, weighing in at around 115 grams. (If you are wondering how heavy this is, go to the shop and pick up a 100-gram bar of chocolate.) The larva will always be bigger than the adult beetle, because all of the ingredients for the adult beetle and energy for metamorphosis are stored inside.

The longest species of beetle is considered to be the Hercules, because of its exceedingly extended horn. But, the beetle with the largest body is undoubtedly the Titan.

It is difficult to know which insect to award the crown of biggest beetle to, but were the regal headdress in my hands, I would place it firmly on the head of the titan, the most intimidating of all Coleoptera.

What about ones with long legs, like the Harlequin?

TITAN BEETLE

(Titanus giganteus)   Family: Cerambycidae

The rarely seen *Titanus giganteus* is a huge Neotropical longhorn beetle, found near the equator in the hot and humid rainforests of Venezuela, Colombia, Ecuador and Brazil.

The beetle's name is derived from the Titans of Greek mythology, who were immortal giants of incredible strength that ruled the world before the gods of Olympus. It is a fierce-looking creature; the largest recorded Titan beetle was almost 17 centimetres long, the size of a small lobster.

DEFENSIVE MEASURES

If threatened, the adult Titan will defend itself by

hissing in warning and biting. If you grabbed it aggressively, the spikes on its legs would make it painful to hold on to, and it is said that its jaws are strong enough to snap a pencil in two, so you might end up with a nasty bite. However, it is rarely aggressive towards humans.

Lucretia Cutter

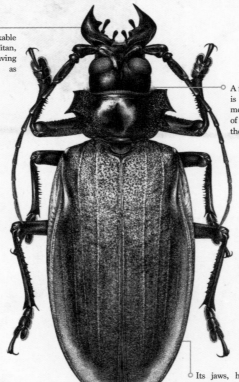

The most remarkable feature of the male Titan, other than its size, is having vicious-looking **jaws** as large as its head.

A fringe of **tiny auburn hair** is visible where the head meets the thorax, and a beard of them can be found around the mandibles and on the legs.

Its jaws, head, long antennae and spiky legs are usually black, whereas the long flat **wing cases** that cover the abdomen are a chestnut brown, tinged with rust.

FIG. 3. TITANUS GIGANTEUS (TITAN BEETLE)

The adult beetle doesn't eat, but rather spends its time looking for a mate, as its purpose is procreation. The Titan is too heavy to take flight from the ground, and so it climbs trees using its spiky legs, and launches itself off high branches to become airborne. When the weather is at its hottest and most humid, Titan beetles fly around following the scent of pheromones, looking for a mate.

The males are attracted to light, and therefore are easily caught in light traps, but the rather sensible females are not. They sit and wait to be discovered by the males and so are extremely hard to find.

LARGE LARVAE

The female Titan lays her eggs in the ground and the larvae feed on dead wood. We have no way of knowing the length of the Titan lifecycle – although they must take years to reach a size large enough to pupate – because no one has ever seen a Titan larva or pupa. This is perhaps because they reach maturity inside tree roots and branches underground. However, boreholes have been discovered that suggest Titan larva can grow up to a staggering thirty centimetres long and five centimetres wide, which is the size of a hefty rolling pin. If a larva were ever to be found and weighed, I'd wager it would be heavier than a Goliath.

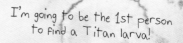

I'm going to be the 1st person to find a Titan larva!

FIG. 4. THE LIFE CYCLE OF A TITAN BEETLE (TITANUS GIGANTEUS)

GOLIATH BEETLE

(Goliathus goliatus)   Family: Scarabaeidae

Goliath beetles are the most famous of the flower beetles. They are named after the biblical giant who was brought down by a boy, David, with a shot from his sling; and they are some of the largest and heaviest insects on Earth, ranging from five to eleven centimetres in size.

DELICIOUS GRUB

Goliath larvae feed on decaying wood and can grow exceedingly large. A fully-grown larva would easily fill the palm of your hand. Despite looking as appetising as uncooked haggis, this giant grub is edible and rich in protein. On one of my visits to Ghana, I witnessed Goliath grubs being prepared for supper. The contents of their guts were squeezed out, rather like a tube of toothpaste, and then they were smoked over a fire and dried out. Fried up with onions, tomatoes and spices they were quite delicious, although you must remember to remove the head before eating.

Ew! GROSS!!!

My oldest friend is an entomologist who I met at university; his name is Hector Dungworthy and he's known throughout Oxford for his love of the herringbone suit, and for sporting an excellently coiffed moustache. He's a methodical scientist and

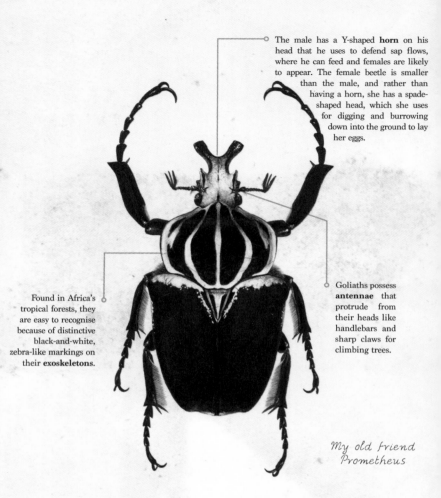

The male has a Y-shaped **horn** on his head that he uses to defend sap flows, where he can feed and females are likely to appear. The female beetle is smaller than the male, and rather than having a horn, she has a spade-shaped head, which she uses for digging and burrowing down into the ground to lay her eggs.

Found in Africa's tropical forests, they are easy to recognise because of distinctive black-and-white, zebra-like markings on their **exoskeletons**.

Goliaths possess **antennae** that protrude from their heads like handlebars and sharp claws for climbing trees.

My old friend Prometheus

FIG. 5. GOLIATHUS GOLIATUS (GOLIATH BEETLE)

wonderful company on field trips, but his passion is breeding and rearing beetles from all over the world. He has an extraordinary glasshouse where he replicates tropical conditions for his exotic beetles. There is no finer way to spend an evening than sat with a bottle of vintage port watching his beetle menagerie. Hector tells me that although the adult beetles live two or three months in the wild, where they have to deal with weather and predators, in captivity they can live for about a year.

FLIGHTS OF FANCY

Despite looking far too heavy to get off the ground, Goliath beetles do fly, high up in the canopy of the forest, and can be mistaken for birds. They launch themselves off branches, and the sight is extraordinary because their wings have a blueish purple iridescence, rather like oil on water.

One evening, when we were putting the world to rights in his glasshouse, Hector told me about a rather curious African Goliath beetle in the collection at the Natural History Museum in London, which has a series of puzzling holes in its exoskeleton. Upon investigation these holes were identified as the entry and exit wounds of gun shot; indeed, an X-ray revealed a shotgun pellet was still inside the unfortunate beetle's body! The position of the wounds showed that the beetle was shot in the back, and Hector believes the beetle must have been performing one of the high aerobatic displays that make Goliaths notoriously difficult to catch, when it was mistaken for a bird and brought down by gunfire.

Prometheus lived for 3 years before showing signs of slowing down. Could this be an effect of my DNA?

FIG. 6. CHALCOSOMA CAUCASUS (RHINOCEROS BEETLE)

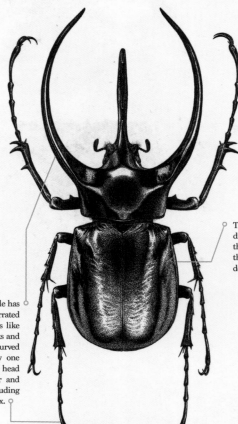

The **exoskeleton** has a distinct metallic lustre that I believe makes it the most dashing and debonair of all beetles.

YES!!!

The rhino beetle has powerful serrated **legs** with claws like grappling hooks and enormous curved **horns,** usually one rising from the head like a scimitar and a pair protruding from the thorax.

RHINOCEROS BEETLE

(Chalcosoma caucasus) Family: Scarabaeidae

Baxter is a messy eater.

(It wasn't me!)

THE TROUBLE WITH NAMES

When it comes to beetles and their common names, you can be forgiven for getting confused. The rhinoceros beetle is a perfect case study. It gets its name because the word 'rhinoceros' comes from the Greek 'rhinokeros' meaning 'nose-horned', and like the mammal, the beetle is a large herbivore with an impressive horn – or at least the male is. However, there are more than one species of beetle with a horn. In fact there are many, and nearly all of them are commonly referred to as rhinoceros beetles.

Rhinoceros beetles can be found on every continent except Antarctica and all hail from the Scarabaeidae family. In the United States of America rhinoceros beetles can be found from northeast Arizona to Nebraska and eastward. *Oryctes nasicornis* – a diminutive cousin to its Neotropical relatives at around four centimetres in size – is known as the European rhino beetle.

To confuse things even further, some rhinoceros beetles have additional common names, such as Atlas, Hercules or elephant beetles. People may say 'the devil is in the detail', but for an entomologist the detail of an invertebrate is where the delight lies, being able to identify a specific species or discover an unrecorded one. The rhinoceros beetle is a great example of why the scientifically accepted, Latinate taxonomy system of naming things is such a wonderful and necessary solution for identifying flora and fauna.

I'm rather fond of

bestowing names – and so, I am going to acknowledge that the rhinoceros beetle can be any of a variety of species of scarab with a horn (or without, if it's female), but in this book I will use it to describe the *Chalcosoma caucasus*, which has been a particular favourite beetle of mine ever since my second expedition to Sumatra, where I met a friendly *caucasus* who took a liking to the banana in my lunch box.

The male *Chalcosoma caucasus* is a large, glossy, black rhinoceros beetle native to Asia, and can be found in Malaysia and Indonesia.

Baxter is from Asia!

The male beetle's horns are hollow and light, so it is able to fly, and it uses them for a variety of tasks: to dig (the beetle is nocturnal and buries itself during the day to escape danger), to forge a path through the jungle leaves littering the forest floor, and of course as weapons in battles against other males, to win the hearts of female rhinoceros beetles.

Baxter only figh bad people/beet

ALL BARK, NO BITE

Despite its ferocious looks, size, strength and armature, the rhinoceros beetle is relatively harmless. If disturbed or frightened by a predator – a snake or a bird – the fearsome appearance of these beetles will be accompanied by a loud hiss in an attempt to ward off an attack. The hissing squeak is a theatrical deceit, caused by the beetle rubbing its abdomen against the ends of its wing cases. This noise-making is called stridulation.

Good for fighting off bullies

The female rhinoceros beetle is smaller than the male, and her elytra are fuzzy; they have a velvety texture. She is more streamlined in shape and has no need for a horn. Her body is designed for digging and moving within the decomposing logs in which she deposits her eggs, hence the strong legs and the sharp claws.

The lifespan of the *Chalcosoma caucasus* is around two years, with the first twelve to eighteen months being in larval form. I found that the *caucasus* who visited my lunch box was partial to melon and cucumber; however, it displayed a definite preference for banana. It hugged the thing to pieces!

! TOO SHORT !

Baxter has human DNA. Will he live longer? ASK DAD

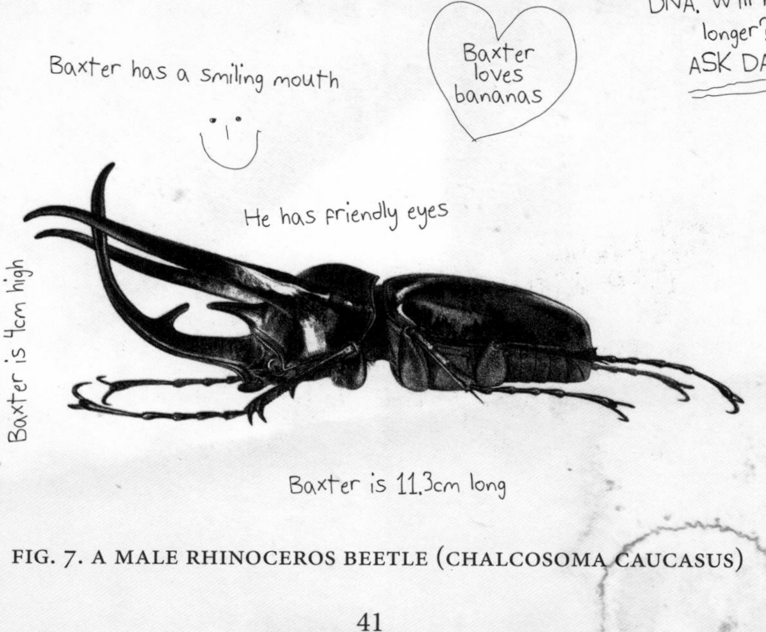

Baxter has a smiling mouth

Baxter loves bananas

He has friendly eyes

Baxter is 4cm high

Baxter is 11.3cm long

FIG. 7. A MALE RHINOCEROS BEETLE (CHALCOSOMA CAUCASUS)

41

ATLAS BEETLE

(Chalcosoma atlas) Family: Scarabaeidae

In Greek mythology, Atlas led the Titans in battle against the Olympian gods for control of the heavens. When the Titans lost, Zeus punished Atlas, by making him bear the weight of the heavens on his shoulders. The Atlas beetle gets its name because of its strength.

STRONG HORN

Rhinoceros beetles are some of the strongest creatures on the planet, relative to their size. I have been at more than a handful of dinners where I've been told by a knowing enthusiast that the rhinoceros beetle

FIG. 8. CHALCOSOMA ATLAS (ATLAS BEETLE)

is able to lift up to eight-hundred-and-fifty times its own weight. This is the equivalent to a man lifting five double-decker buses!

WOW!!

Superman only lifts one bus!!

Now, it is true that these beetles are phenomenally strong, but I was curious to discover where this number of eight-hundred-and-fifty came from. I'm afraid to say that my detective skills are not as finely honed as those of Sherlock Holmes. Try as I might, I have not been able to find the source of this claim. Whilst sleuthing, I read about this chap (Rodger Kram) at the University of California who carried out an experiment with rhino beetles by putting them on a small insect treadmill and adding weights to their backs, gradually increasing the burden, to see what was the maximum load the beetles could carry whilst still moving forward. He found the rhinoceros beetle was able to carry a hundred times its body mass and still walk, although not steadily. This is an incredible exhibition of strength. I wonder if perhaps the experiment that led to the 'eight-hundred-and-fifty times its body weight' claim was a different kind of test. For example if you trapped an Atlas beetle beneath a weight, how heavy would the object have to be before the beetle couldn't lift it and escape? Sadly, I don't have the answer to this question.

HAHA!

I could do this with Baxter. I don't want to squash him, though.

SPOT THE DIFFERENCE

The *Chalcosoma atlas* is closely related to

the *Chalcosoma caucasus* (which is, rather confusingly, sometimes called the Great Atlas Beetle). They are both to be found in southern Asia, in Indonesia and Malaysia. They both eat sap and rotting fruit, are remarkable in size and strength, and have imposing horns. However, the Atlas is smaller and its wing cases are usually more bronze in colour than the darker blue of the *caucasus*. The other difference between the two beetles is in the shape of the horns sprouting from their heads, which on the Atlas broadens and has an upward-curving, hook-like section with distinct raised ridges.

NIPPERS WHO NIP

The Atlas larvae can exhibit fierce behaviour, biting if touched, and I was once told that if they live together in too close a proximity they will fight to the death for food. This behaviour is unusual amongst herbivores, although I've certainly been nibbled by many different types of larvae over the years.

It doesn't hurt.
Like a pinprick.

FIG. 9. DYNASTES HERCULES (HERCULES BEETLE)

There can be no doubt that the male Hercules beetle is a handsome beast. Its imposing horned **head** is mahogany-brown, almost black, with a pair of berry-like **eyes** either side of its head **horn**.

The **elytra** of the Hercules are a stunning golden brown and usually freckled with dark spots.

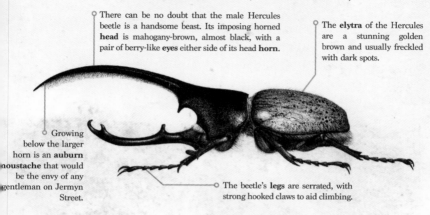

Growing below the larger horn is an **auburn moustache** that would be the envy of any gentleman on Jermyn Street.

The beetle's **legs** are serrated, with strong hooked claws to aid climbing.

HERCULES BEETLE

(Dynastes hercules) Family: Scarabaeidae

Hercules beetles *(Dynastes hercules)* are one of the most beloved and well known species of all the giant beetles. They appear in scientific records from hundreds of years ago. In classical mythology, Hercules is famous for his strength, and I'm sure by now you've spotted the trend in the naming of these colossal beasts. Humans have always been fascinated by the extraordinary strength of giant beetles.

The male Hercules beetle can measure up to seventeen centimetres in length (including its horn), which makes it one of the longest insects in the world and possibly the largest beetle. It is native to the rainforests of Central America, South America and the Lesser Antilles. Like its cousins, the adult beetle eats rotting fruit whilst its larvae feed on decaying wood, and the female is the smaller, hornless and hairier of the two sexes.

READY FOR BATTLE

The most distinctive feature of the male Hercules beetle is the enormous horn that extends from its thorax, which is mirrored by a horn sprouting from its head. The head horn can be moved upward, against the longer, downward-curving thorax horn, rather like the claw of a crab or a lobster. It uses its horns in battle with other males, first rearing up to show off its weaponry in a display of intimidation, then parrying, jousting and grabbing its opponent around the thorax in a pincer-like grasp and tossing him aside.

SPIRACLES

FIG. 10. A HERCULES BEETLE (DYNASTES HERCULES) LARVA

FIG. 11. MEGASOMA ELEPHAS (ELEPHANT BEETLE)

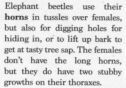

Elephant beetles use their **horns** in tussles over females, but also for digging holes for hiding in, or to lift up bark to get at tasty tree sap. The females don't have the long horns, but they do have two stubby growths on their thoraxes.

The elephant beetle is black, but covered with a thick carpet of tiny **mustard-yellow hairs**, which make it appear a burnt orange colour.

ELEPHANT BEETLE

(Megasoma elephas) Family: Scarabaeidae

Take one look at the *Megasoma elephas* and you will see how it got its name. It has a long horn rising from its head that ends in a Y-shape, like a trumpeting trunk, and two stubby tusk-like horns on its thorax. It grows to about twelve centimetres; the male will be at least twice the size of the female. Hector Dungworthy says his elephant beetles are partial to pineapple and lychees, but in the wild they eat tree-sap and fallen fruit.

The elephant beetle likes warm climates and can be found living in the tropical forests of southern Mexico and Central and South America. The beetles make their homes in trees, and some females lay their eggs high up in the canopy, in holes or empty bird's-nests – where the larvae will be protected from predators – but most will lay eggs in the rotting wood on the ground. The larvae eat dead wood and can take up to three years to grow big enough to pupate.

Sadly, there is a fashion in Nicaragua, Costa Rica and other countries in Central America for wearing the elephant beetle's head – smothered in gold – as a charm necklace, and this has affected the population severely.

GIANTS IN DANGER

All of these incredibly impressive beetles live in rainforests. As humans cut down trees for palm oil and logging, or drill the land for oil, these habitats are disappearing and the giant beetles are becoming endangered.

Insects are very successful breeders, and where they have the habitat they need, they are numerous. The real damage to a species is done when we deprive them of the habitat in which they live, eat and breed. And if we wish to continue to share this planet with colossal Coleoptera, we must protect the rainforests of this world with all our might.

YES!!!

BORING
BEETLES

Of course it is impossible for a beetle to be boring! But, I would like to introduce you to a battalion of beetles capable of bringing your house down. I'll bet you've already heard of woodworm, and perhaps you assumed the creature to be a worm, but the name refers to the larvae of wood-boring beetles. Larvae are hungry little beasts, and they live inside wood, gouging out tiny tunnels as they eat and grow. They stop eating to pupate and once they've become adult beetles they chew their way to freedom, leaving holes in the surface of the wood.

It is almost impossible to know you have a woodworm problem until it is too late. People spot the cavities and treat them with insecticide to kill the beetles, but the holes mean that the beetles have already bolted. The holes in your grandparents' furnishings were probably made by the common furniture beetle, *Anobium punctatum*, but there are many other boring beetles.

It's still CRUEL!

49

Has anyone ever called you a bookworm – a charming term for one who loves to read? But, it is also the nickname for the larvae of certain beetles, who, rather criminally, are partial to devouring old books!

In small quantities, wood-boring beetles do much good, eating away at weak and dying trees, recycling wood and making space for new growth. But, if a population of beetles grows too large they can <u>destroy entire forests,</u> or turn that chair you're sitting in to sawdust.

LONGHORN BEETLE

(Petrognatha gigas) Family: Cerambycidae

A longhorn beetle is characterised by the length of its impressive antennae, which can be as long or longer than its body. Antennae perform a similar function to noses, and sit in a similar place on a beetle's head, sticking out beneath its eyes. My dear friend Hector has what we call a Roman nose. It protrudes proudly over his magnificent moustache, but even his conk is no equal to the longhorn's feelers. These extraordinary antennae give the beetle its common name, but the scientific name of the longhorn beetle family comes from a character in Greek mythology called Cerambus. He was Poseidon's grandson, and foolish enough to get into an argument with the nymphs, who subsequently transformed him into a wood-gnawing beetle with

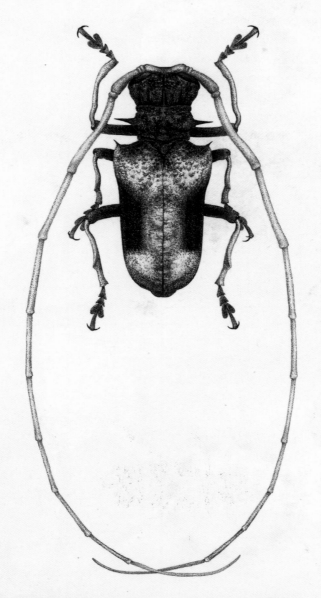

WHOA!
Thats a
big nose.

FIG. 12. PETROGNATHA GIGAS (LONGHORN BEETLE)

51

horns. Lesson learned, I should think!

The longhorn family is large, with over twenty-six thousand species found all over the world. Some of them are pests, but not all longhorns are destructive.

LYING LONGHORN

One of my favourite British longhorn beetles is the wasp beetle, *Clytus arietis*. To deter predators from eating it, this beetle imitates a wasp in size, shape and colouration, and flies from flower to flower feeding on nectar. You'll need keen eyes if you are to tell the beetle mimic from the real wasp, but of course the difference is in the wings. It can be spotted by the observant beetle collector between the months of May and July, but take care not to try and pick one up until you are sure it's the harmless beetle!

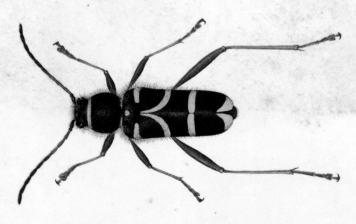

FIG. 13. CLYTUS ARIETIS (WASP BEETLE)

OLD HOUSE BORER

(*Hylotrupes bajulus*) Family: Cerambycidae

The old house borer, *Hylotrupes bajulus*, is a European beetle that has spread across the globe, travelling with the expanding human population. The ravenous grubs are pale as porcelain, with sharp, black jaws. Their favourite food is timber rich with resin, a sap-like substance exuded by trees when injured. They adore freshly cut softwood, like pine, but, if wood is old, with less resin, then the larvae have to eat much more of it before they can pupate, which is how they got their name.

Many historical houses have had to replace

FIG. 15. HYLOTRUPES BAJULUS (OLD HOUSE BORER)

structural beams that have been almost entirely eaten away by beetles, or risk collapse. The journey from egg to adult can take up to ten years of tunnelling, depending on the type of wood the larva is eating.

Next time you are visiting an old building with exposed beams, look up and see if you can spot the beetle holes. You'll soon realise they're everywhere. Another house pest is the powderpost beetle, which likes starchy hardwoods such as oak or mahogany, and if you're really unlucky they will munch away at your windows, doorframes and floors, whilst the old house borer takes care of your structural beams. *This gives me an idea*

Show Bertolt

GHOSTLY GOBBLING

The larvae of the old house borer would never be invited to dine at the club because they're such noisy eaters. Their strong jaws chew away at the wood making a clicking sound that can be heard by the residents of the house they're consuming. Hector and I once spent a blissful week on Dartmoor, hunting for the elusive blue ground beetle, *Carabus intricatus*, which is Britain's largest, but rarely seen, carabid. We stayed at a delightfully eccentric place called the Highwayman Inn, which dates back to 1282, and at dinner we were regaled with tales of the ghosts and spirits that inhabit the old building. I love a good ghost story as much as the next person, but as I was enjoying my steak and ale pie I noticed the wooden beams of the building were scarred with polka dot holes. I suspect the noisy crunchings of the old house borer might have been the cause of one or two of the ghost stories coming out of the woodwork that night.

Good for frightening people

———————— ∽ ————————

FIG. 15. ANTHRENUS VERBASCI (CARPET BEETLE)

CARPET BEETLE

(Anthrenus verbasci) Family: Dermestidae

I'm hardly a trend-setter. My uniform of three-piece Harris tweed suits never varies. They are acceptable at the club, comfortable in my study, and practical when out on a field trip. Hector has suggested I purchase a pair of plus fours (shorts that extend below the knee) for outdoor work, but whilst he cuts a dashing figure in his, with his tall and slender frame, they make me look like a chubby schoolboy who's lost his cap. Our next beetle feels the same way I do about tweed.

The larvae of the carpet beetle, *Anthrenus verbasci*, feeds on clothing, blankets and carpets. Throughout Europe and the northern hemisphere, the adult beetles fly in through open windows in the summer and lay their eggs on natural fibres. You may not know you've been visited until you find holes in your rug or your jumper, although they don't generally cause too much damage.

The larvae are so hairy themselves that they're known as woolly bears. My mother used to tell me that woolly bears were responsible for eating the holes in my school scarf, and it was many years before I realised what she meant, and that she wasn't losing her marbles!

BANNED FROM THE MUSEUM

The museum beetle, *Anthrenus museorum*, is a cousin of the carpet beetle and a menace wherever taxidermy creatures are displayed. I can find something nice to say about almost any beetle, but I struggle with this little terror, because any collection stored or put away for long periods of time is at risk of becoming their dinner. They eat dry skin and exoskeletons. The insatiable larvae are tiny, at around four millimetres long, and the adult beetle is even smaller, making it difficult to spot.

When I began collecting beetles, I kept my specimens in cardboard collection boxes. One day, when I wanted to transfer my growing collection into a beautiful set of wooden drawers, I lifted the lid of the first box I'd ever built, only to find that the museum beetles had paid it a visit. What was once a neatly laid out box of pinned beetles, each accompanied by a label, was a mess of empty pins, dust and hollow, headless exoskeletons. The larvae had eaten the poor beetles from the inside out and finished off the labels for dessert. I'm not ashamed to admit that I wept at the sight, knowing that I could never go back in time, to Ecuador, and get those samples back.

IKES!

BARK BEETLE

(*S c o l y t u s   s c o l y t u s*) Family: Curculionidae

As I'm sure you've already guessed, bark beetles feed on the bark of trees. They are a type of weevil (see page 74) found all over the world. Most species live in dead or dying trees. They help create a diverse forest ecosystem, and habitats for other insects and fungi, by killing off older trees, clearing areas for new growth. Healthy young trees defend themselves by oozing fresh resin, a sticky substance the tree produces to trap and suffocate attacking insects.

FIG. 16. SCOLYTUS SCOLYTUS (ELM BARK BEETLE)

LETHAL LUMBERJACKS

If a tree has a bark beetle problem, you will see a pattern on the trunk, as the larvae's tunnels scar it. Bark beetles are terrifying pests in large numbers. They increase the risk of forest fires by making trees weak in times of drought, and if the population of a single species explodes, it can wipe out an entire woodland or type of tree. In the north of America the mountain pine beetle has destroyed millions of hectares of forest, and, in a bid to control the beetle, thousands more trees have had to be chopped down. In Britain, *Scolytus scolytus*, the large elm bark beetle, has killed over sixty million elm trees. It eats away at the bark, introducing a fungal disease, which blocks the tree's efforts to transport water.

FIG. 17. XESTOBIUM RUFOVILLOSUM (DEATHWATCH BEETLE)

The deathwatch beetle's head sits below a hood-like thorax, with which it hammers against wood like a pogoing percussionist, hoping to attract a mate.

Considering its doom-laden name, the physical appearance of the deathwatch beetle is underwhelming. It is a tiny brown speckled creature that blends in with its wooden habitat, and can be at most seven millimetres in length.

DEATHWATCH BEETLE

(Xestobium rufovillosum) Family: Anobiidae

When the grim reaper comes knocking, you may want to pause a moment and consider whether it really is time to shuffle off this mortal coil, or if the sound is a lonely beetle looking for love. The deathwatch beetle, *Xestobium rufovillosum*, found in Europe and eastern North America, is famous for its

ACTUAL SIZE: UP TO 0.7 cm

mating dance, in which it repeatedly head-butts wooden surfaces in a rapid pattern, like a crazed goat, to attract females. This is not a winning strategy for human males.

I once tried to demonstrate the deathwatch beetle's behaviour at a high tea, using the table, and not only did I give myself a sore forehead, but Hector had to apologise profusely to our host, the Duchess of Devonshire, and I have never been invited back.

The deathwatch beetle eats wood and inhabits the damp or decaying softwood found in buildings with poor drainage. When the world was lit by

SCARY NOISES

candles, the sound of this tiny beetle's mating dance took on an eerie quality. The mysterious knocking coming from inside the walls of a house was thought to signify the approach of death, which is how such a tiny and frankly adorable little beetle got such a fear-inducing name.

NIGHT LIGHTS

Which beetle is the most enchanting and enigmatic of them all? Well, if magic is what you are searching for then may I recommend hunting late on summer evenings for the beetles that glow in the dark? The tiny beacon belonging to the firefly looks like a spark from a falling star, and if you happen upon a constellation, the beauty of their twilight dance will take your breath away. The fire beetle, genus *Pyrophorus*, found in parts of South America and the West Indies, produces a dazzling blue-green streak of light when it flies, and it lays its eggs in termite mounds. One mound can be home to so many luminous larvae that the whole structure glows like a star-encrusted meteorite, fallen to earth.

There are a number of beetles that are bioluminescent, which means their bodies can produce light naturally, through a chemical reaction involving an enzyme with the rather sinister name luciferase. They are the shining luminaries of this planet's Coleoptera, the delightful night lights.

———— ～ ————

FIREFLY

(P h o t i n u s   p y r a l i s) Family: Lampyridae

There are about two thousand species of firefly spread across the globe, and most of them use their light to attract a mate or lure in prey. The Greeks of old called the firefly the *bright-tailed*, in Latin it is hailed as the *lantern bearer* and around the world it is commonly known as a lightning bug. All of these names suit these flickering, flashing beetles. Its larvae are glow-worms because they too emit light, and even the eggs of this beetle shine. Fireflies can be found all over the world in temperate or tropical climates, usually in wet and woody areas, and they are nocturnal creatures.

LIGHT SHOW   Show Bertolt

Depending on the species, the light a firefly emits can be yellow, green, pale red or, as with the blue ghost firefly found in the Southern Appalachians in America, an eerie bluish-white. They control

IT'S NEWTON!

A firefly can be up to three centimetres in length and tends to be a copper brown, with leathery elytra and a charming pink thorax.

Its light organ is found in the last two or three segments of its lower abdomen.

FIG. 18. PHOTINUS PYRALIS (FIREFLY)

their glow by adding or withholding oxygen from their light organ. When there's no oxygen the lamp goes out. Female fireflies recognise the male of their own species because each puts on a unique display of flashing patterns, and studies have shown that the flashier the firefly, the more attractive they are to the ladies.

LUMINARIES' LIFECYCLE

A day or two after mating, a female firefly will lay her eggs on or just below the ground. The eggs will hatch after three or four weeks and the larvae will eat until the end of the summer. Before winter comes they find cosy spots in which to hibernate, perhaps underground or beneath the bark of a tree. When spring arrives they emerge and prey on other insects, snails and worms, getting ready to pupate. Their transformation can take up to two-and-a-half weeks, but then they flare into our night skies, dancing and dazzling for all they're worth, until they find a partner.

DEADLY DINERS

Fireflies are foul tasting and most predators avoid them. If a bird or bat inadvertently swallows one it'll bring it back up, and if a lizard accidentally eats one it may die, because the firefly can be poisonous. The light works as a warning to predators not to eat the beetles, although they don't get off entirely scot-free: a toad or a spider will happily prey upon them. The fireflies themselves are omnivores and their diets vary according to species. Some feed on pollen or nectar, but the European glow-worm, *Lampyris noctiluca*, has a ghastly manner of dining which should delight any gardener, because it loves nothing more than a menu of a common garden mollusc. Yes, it eats snails. No garlic or butter needed for the firefly; it consumes snails like a vampire. When the firefly fancies some cold mollusc broth, the sly hunter finds a snail and administers an anaesthetic using <u>two fangs.</u> The unfortunate creature doesn't realise it's about to become supper. Then the beetle injects a poison into the snail, turning its body to a soup that the firefly slurps up with relish, leaving nothing but a shell.

No way! Newton is a snail vampire?!

GLOW-WORM MUDDLE

The term 'glow-worm' is used to describe the luminous larvae of the firefly, but it is also the common name for Phengodidae, a different family to the firefly. To add further confusion, in some species of firefly the females are flightless, and are only distinguishable from larvae because they have compound eyes. Often flightless female fireflies glow fiercely and so they too are called glow-worms.

Always wondered what a glow-worm was.

The glow-worm beetle is from a different family to the firefly (see previous page) and can be found throughout the western hemisphere from southern Canada to Chile. The wingless ladies and their larvae have the light, whereas, if the males glow at all, they glow weakly. Instead they are drawn to the dazzling radiance of the female. Female glow-worms and their larvae eat millipedes and other arthropods found in the soil or leaf litter. She is much larger than the winged male, who will have a brief life and probably not eat at all.

The female's light organs
run down the sides of the
abdominal segments, like tiny
glowing windows in a train
carriage, glowing yellow or
green.

FIG. 19. LAMPYRIS NOCTILUCA (MALE & FEMALE GLOW-WORM)

PRESERVE THE MAGIC

Fireflies and glow-worms are disappearing from the world, almost certainly because of human behaviour. Our spreading populations, pesticides and light pollution are upsetting the lifecycles of these magical creatures. If you wish to help nurture fireflies, here are some simple things you can do:

✓ 1) Leave grass long. Fireflies climb up it to flash and attract mates.

✓ 2) Turn off outside lights at night. Fireflies find their mates by reading light signals. They cannot tell the difference between an electric light and a female firefly, and the flood of artificial light at night-time means they cannot see one another's light signals. This stops them from mating, meaning fewer fireflies are born each year.

✓ 3) Don't have a tidy garden. Let log piles and leaf mulch build up in corners, to make a welcoming home for firefly larvae to live in.

✓ 4) Build a wildlife pond. Fireflies love to live around standing water. Even a small pond can attract the dazzling night dancers, because they eat the insects and snails that thrive in this habitat.

✓ 5) Please don't use pesticides. This will help all wildlife, not just fireflies.

These are easy to do.

THE
UNDERTAKERS

Are you filled with horror at the image of insects eating the flesh of the dead? You really shouldn't be, because if there were no creatures recycling dead bodies, corpses would litter the landscape and disease would be rife. We need the insect undertakers to return the dead to the earth from which they came. The beetles that do this job are fascinating and have even been known to help Scotland Yard with their enquiries. In forensic science, insects point to important clues, such as the time since death, and this helps the police to solve crimes. For example the last scavengers to visit and feed on a dead creature will usually be the warty-looking hide beetles. They eat feathers, hooves, fur and skin. These chaps are sometimes put to work in museums, stripping skeletons of remaining dried skin or flesh, cleaning them for display. Whilst

Nope!

Sherlock Beetle & Weevil!

museums love them, orchestras hate them; hide beetles have been known to sneak into violin cases and banquet on the bows.

I should warn you not to read this section at the dinner table. This bunch of beetles might upset anyone with a weak stomach, but, if you're ready, it's time to visit the undertakers.

Not me

BURYING BEETLE

(Nicrophorus vespilloides) Family: Silphidae

Burying beetles, or sexton beetles as they are sometimes called, are carrion beetles, which means they feed on the decaying flesh of dead animals. They are scavengers that bury the dead bodies of small birds and rodents, because for the burying beetle a cadaver is the perfect home and food supply for its new family. These beetles can be found in most parts of the world, and in England they can be spotted between the months of April and October.

A FAMILY BUSINESS

Burying beetles are unusual because both parents take care of their children. They work together, digging around and below the corpse of a dead bird

70

Burying beetles are between one- and two-and-a-half centimetres in length and have shovel-shaped heads for digging.

Their sensitive antennae have comb-like ends to help them detect the whiff of death from a mile away.

Pattern looks like an evil bat signal!

Their bodies are a glossy black, and most species have orange or red markings on their elytra, which are a little shorter than their abdomens.

Oh my goodness, it's LENKA!!!

FIG. 20. NICROPHORUS VESPILLOIDES (BURYING BEETLE)

71

or a mouse, hiding it in an unmarked grave from other hungry scavengers. The next thing they do is revolting: The beetles chew off the hair or feathers of the dead creature and use that material to make a chamber, a little house for their family, above or beside the carcass. Then they spit or wipe their bottoms all over the cadaver, covering it with an embalming fluid, to stop it from rotting. The female lays her eggs in the chamber, and, when the larvae hatch, the parents call their children over with a chirping sound, feeding them bite-sized chunks of the deceased until they have grown big enough to feed themselves.

If disturbed, some species will let off a really strong pong of rotting flesh to put a predator off eating them.

CLOWN BEETLE

(Hister quadrimaculatus) Family: Histeridae

Despite their cheerful name, clown beetles (also called hister beetles) are macabre little devils. They hide during the day under a corpse – or inside it, if it is rotten – and at night they venture out to raid the corpse and devour the fly eggs and maggots feeding there. They are carnivorous predators and will even eat other clown beetles, so if you are detaining them for more careful study, make sure you put them in separate containers. It is

Maggot munchers

FIG. 21. HISTER QUADRIMACULATUS (CLOWN BEETLE)

a delicious irony that if frightened these beetles will pretend to be dead.

Clown beetles have proved useful to the police in forensic investigations because they don't arrive at a corpse until there is something to feed on, and they are only active at night. Added to this is the information we have about their speedy life cycle. Within twenty days an egg can transform into an adult beetle. Using this information helps detectives estimate the time of death of a corpse.

INCONCEIVABLE WEEVILS

Weevils have mouthparts for chewing and a pair of sheathed wings, which makes them beetles. Their heads are roughly the same shape as an anteater's, which makes them seem like comedic characters, but because most weevils feed on plants, seeds or grain, they are largely considered pests.

There are over <u>sixty thousand species of weevil</u> in the Curculionoidea superfamily, making them the single largest group of creatures on the planet. It would be possible to write a book purely about the wonder of weevils, but instead I'm going to introduce you to a few whose existence is both astounding and preposterous.

GIRAFFE-NECKED WEEVIL

(Trachelophorus giraffa) Family: Attelabidae

The giraffe-necked weevil, *Trachelophorus giraffa*, lives in Madagascar. It can only be found on one particular type of tree, which is known as the giraffe beetle tree. The weevil gets its name from the odd shape of its body, which resembles a giraffe's, and, despite the ridiculous neck, this weevil can fly.

WEIRD WEAPON

The long neck is a weapon for fighting. Male giraffe-necked weevils will duel one another on a leaf or branch, by walloping their challengers with their own heads until they knock them off. The weevil with the strongest, longest neck usually wins the fight and therefore a lady weevil's affections. The female beetle has a much shorter neck, but stronger, more bulbous legs, which she uses to fold a leaf around her egg, creating a protective nest before then dropping it to the forest floor.

Ha Ha!

The giraffe-necked weevil's neck extends up and then forward, like an angle-poised lamp, tipped with a bobble of a head and serrated antennae that always make me think of Salvador Dali's moustache.

It is a comparatively large weevil, at up to three centimetres in length, although most of that is 'neck'. It has a coffee-bean-shaped body with pillar-box-red elytra.

Such a DUDE

FIG. 22. TRACHELOPHORUS GIRAFFA (GIRAFFE-NECKED WEEVIL)

BLUE WEEVIL

(E u p h o l u s   m a g n i f i c u s)   Family: Curculionidae

Of all the weevils on the planet, the blue weevil, *Eupholus magnificus*, has to be one of the most striking. This handsome beast hails from New Guinea and is very popular with exotic insect collectors. It lives in tropical rainforests, feeding on yam leaves. It is thought that the crazy riot of blue on these beetles' exoskeletons may be a warning to predators that they are not good to eat, because yam leaves are poisonous to some creatures.

The combination of the long elbowed antennae, the toddling walk on padded claws and the vibrant colour and pattern of the blue weevil's body makes me chortle with delight; I think of this beetle as the Charlie Chaplin of the weevil world.

The rainbow of electric blues and turquoise across the blue weevil's body come from tiny scales that reflect light. Where the weevil's wing cases are black, there is an absence of these scales.

FIG. 23. EUPHOLUS MAGNIFICUS (BLUE WEEVIL)

WHEAT WEEVIL

(S i t o p h i l u s   g r a n a r i u s)   Family: Dryophthoridae

The wheat weevil, *Sitophilus granarius*, is found all over the world. This common pest can destroy the crop yields of wheat, oats, rye, barley, rice and corn, and it also damages stored grain.

ACTUAL SIZE: UP TO 0.5 cm

It's not just farmers that hate these weevils. These tiny pests can eat through plastic and paper bags, as well as cardboard. If you don't store your food in tightly sealed glass or metal containers then you may find a population of wheat weevils taking up residence in your pantry. My mother would place little cloth pouches of peppercorns in our pantry to repel the weevils, although I'm not certain how much that helped.

LUCRETIA'S ARMY

DIMINUTIVE DESTROYER

The wheat weevil does an extraordinary amount of damage to human food; if a storage facility is infested, <u>all of the grain has to be destroyed.</u>

Each female can lay hundreds of eggs. She chews a hole in a grain and inserts a single egg, then seals the hole with a jelly-like ooze. The entire life cycle of the wheat weevil takes place inside the grain kernel over two months. After pupation the weevil pops out of the grain, living for eight months, looking for a mate to lay eggs. <u>One pair of weevils</u> can produce up to <u>six thousand young</u> in a year.

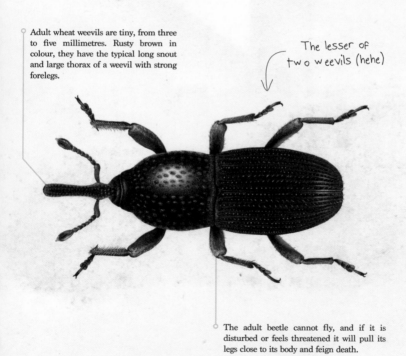

Adult wheat weevils are tiny, from three to five millimetres. Rusty brown in colour, they have the typical long snout and large thorax of a weevil with strong forelegs.

The lesser of two weevils (hehe)

The adult beetle cannot fly, and if it is disturbed or feels threatened it will pull its legs close to its body and feign death.

FIG. 24. SITOPHILUS GRANARIUS (WHEAT WEEVIL)

MASSIVE MANDIBLES

Beetles that possess mammoth mandibles are imposing figures and are at their most impressive when they are readying for a fight. Like two jousting knights they line up opposite one another and perform an intimidating display of rising up on to their back legs, lifting their front legs wide and showing off the size of their jaws. Then they march steadfastly towards each other to fight in jaw-to-jaw combat for the attentions of a lady.

Some beetles have jaws and claws that could rival the fabled Jabberwocky. Their mandibles can extend up to ten times the size of their heads. These creatures are not designed for refined dining. I chuckle to think of the dinner parties were our jaws as large as those of the stag beetle; our chins would be dragging on the floor!

STAG BEETLE

(Lucanus cervus) Family: Lucanidae

Stag beetles are the largest and most impressive looking insects in Europe. *Lucanus cervus* were once to be found right across the continent, but are becoming a rare sight. I count my blessings that there's a thriving population in south London, as I get to observe these magnificent beasts every summer. They get their common name from their jaws, which resemble the antlers of a stag. In the past they have had other names, such as thunder beetle or horse pincher, but I think stag beetle suits them best. ← Naff

Although the male appears to have horns or antlers, these impressive appendages are their mouthparts, their mandibles, with which they wrestle other male stag beetles. Despite looking so fierce, these magnificent creatures are not harmful to humans. You are more likely to get a nip from the female, which has less impressive jaws but is speedier of foot. She is much quicker to bite if she's scared. The milky-white stag larvae are large, growing up to eleven centimetres in length. You will find them buried in the ground beneath rotting wood piles, and they can be recognised by their orange heads and brown jaws.

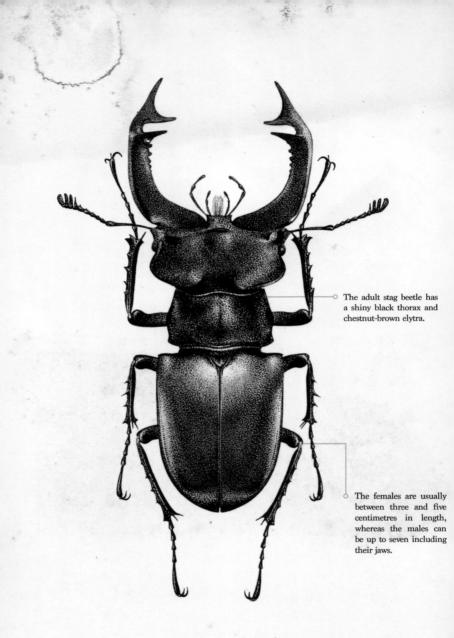

The adult stag beetle has a shiny black thorax and chestnut-brown elytra.

The females are usually between three and five centimetres in length, whereas the males can be up to seven including their jaws.

FIG. 25. LUCANUS CERVUS (STAG BEETLE)

Stag beetles have become harder to find in England because of the loss of woodland habitat and the fashion for tidy gardens. *Lucanus cervus* is now an endangered species and sightings are rare in northern England; it is not found at all in Ireland. This is a cause of great sadness to me; if you see one, you should consider yourself very fortunate.

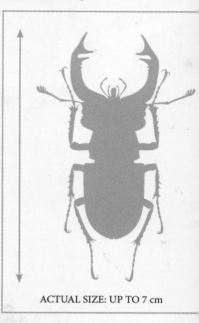

ACTUAL SIZE: UP TO 7 cm

These beetles can be found at the edges of woodland, in orchards or parks. The adult beetle barely eats, although it may drink from fallen fruit or tree sap. The females like to lay eggs in soil in which it is easy to dig, so won't be found in chalky or clay areas.

INTERNATIONAL STAG PARTY

There are over one thousand two hundred species of stag beetle to be found across the world, and all are impressive-looking beasts. They range in size from 0.6 to twelve centimetres. There are some grand-looking chaps in Asia and at least thirty species in the United States of America, but my favourite of all of them are the rainbow stags from Australia, *Phalacrognathus muelleri*. The male can be anything up to seven centimetres in length and has an upward-curving pair of jaws. Both male and female have a golden thorax and iridescent elytra. They really are very pretty, and they also make good companions, because they live as adults for up to eighteen months, which is a lot longer than the poor British stag (see below).

UNDERGROUND EXISTENCE

A British stag beetle lives most of its life in larval form, underground, sometimes as deep as fifty centimetres below the surface. It can spend up to five years as a larva, eating rotting wood, and emerge from its pupa in late spring as an adult beetle, digging its way to the surface. You will see these beetles flying about at dusk, searching for mates. After a holiday romance of five or six weeks, the adult beetles die (if they don't get eaten first). They are preyed upon by birds of all sorts, and foxes will eat them too. The domestic cat will harass the poor creatures to death for fun.

So long!

DARWIN BEETLE

(Chiasognathus grantii) Family: Lucanidae

The male Darwin's beetle, *Chiasognathus grantii*, has, comparatively, got the biggest jaws of all creatures. And, despite their unwieldiness, can still fly.

This species of stag beetle is found in Argentina and Chile and was named after Charles Darwin, *Total hero* who collected and wrote about the species during the second voyage of the *HMS Beagle*. Despite the beetle having gigantic mandibles, Darwin noted that the jaws were 'not so strong as to produce pain to finger', and this is because they are not used for biting but fighting. The beetle climbs tall trees and uses its massive jaws to fight off other males as they compete for a mate.

Darwin's beetles vary in size: the male can be anything up to nine centimetres in length, whereas the female is between two and four centimetres long. The female is shorter because she doesn't have the extended jaws.

Sadly, this is a rare and vulnerable species of beetle with a high probability of extinction because the climate of the world is changing.

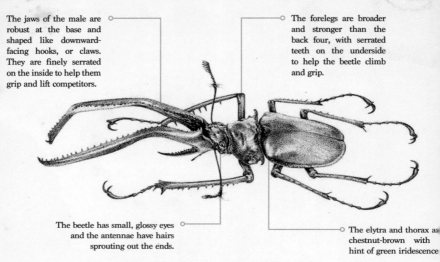

The jaws of the male are robust at the base and shaped like downward-facing hooks, or claws. They are finely serrated on the inside to help them grip and lift competitors.

The forelegs are broader and stronger than the back four, with serrated teeth on the underside to help the beetle climb and grip.

The beetle has small, glossy eyes and the antennae have hairs sprouting out the ends.

The elytra and thorax are chestnut-brown with hint of green iridescence

FIG. 26. CHIASOGNATHUS GRANTII (DARWIN'S BEETLE)

FIGHTING FOR LOVE

The female *Chiasognathus grantii* is to be found high up on a tree trunk, sometimes twenty metres up in the canopy, feeding on sap. The male will climb using his claws and frequently encounter other males doing the same thing. They will go into battle, trying to hook their jaws over each other, aiming to get them under their competitor's wing covers. Usually the male with the biggest jaws will succeed, close his jaws and attempt to lift the other beetle from the branch. The vulnerable beetle will hook his claws into the branch and cling on.

The treetop battles of Darwin's beetles are extraordinary. The winner will eventually pry his opponent off the tree and drop him to the forest floor. He will bounce, protected by his exoskeleton, and begin the climb back up. A male may have to fight many times before he reaches a female.

But there the chivalry ends. Once the pair have successfully mated, the male will toss his erstwhile partner to the forest floor too, where she will lay her eggs.

TIGER BEETLE

(*Cicindela campestris*)   Family: Carabidae

If I asked you to name some of the fastest creatures on the planet, would a beetle spring to mind? If not, then you can't have met the tiger beetle. Tiger beetles are athletes. *Cicindela hudsoni* is able to run one hundred and twenty five body lengths per second. By comparison the best Olympic sprinters can only run five body lengths per second. To match the tiger beetle, they would need to run five hundred miles per hour!

Super speed

Tiger beetles are a large group, with over two-and-a-half-thousand species spread across the world. They thrive in sandy soils and open, bare ground, and so are found beside the sea, lakes, on heaths, hillsides or woodland paths.

SETTING A TRAP

The green tiger beetle, *Cicindela campestris*, is

common in Britain. It feeds on small invertebrates including spiders, caterpillars and ants, and it breeds in the summer, laying its eggs in small burrows in the ground. When the eggs hatch the larvae stay in the burrow, using it like a pitfall trap, waiting for passing prey. The unsuspecting target either falls in, or, if it tries to escape, the larvae will dart out and grab it, dragging it into the tunnel to eat.

While the adult females look very similar to the males, their larvae look a bit like pale oriental dragons: each has a large, dark, flat head with vicious mandibles, six strong legs and the white caterpillar-like bodies of most larvae. It has a hunched back with hooks to anchor it to the side of its burrow.

It is not an easy thing to catch such a fast beetle – you'll have to be quick! And remember: it can also fly.

HAZARDOUS HUNTERS

Tiger beetles need speed for hunting prey, but they run so fast that their vision becomes a blur and they can't see. They have to sprint in short bursts, orientating themselves when they stop. It causes me no end of mirth that such a vicious hunter loses sight of its prey as soon as it dashes towards it. Even more wonderful *Ha Ha* is the zigzag pattern in which the tiger beetle moves, as it often has to change course, once it has had a look about, to catch its quarry.

Tiger beetles have an ingenious way of overcoming the obstacles they fail to see. To avoid

The green tiger beetle's wing cases are spotted with cream patches and it has spindly legs and straight antennae.

It has bottle-green elytra, thorax and head.

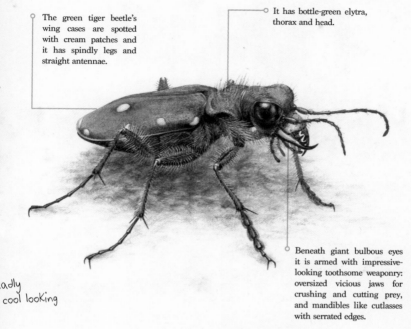

Beneath giant bulbous eyes it is armed with impressive-looking toothsome weaponry: oversized vicious jaws for crushing and cutting prey, and mandibles like cutlasses with serrated edges.

deadly cool looking

FIG. 27. CICINDELA CAMPESTRIS (TIGER BEETLE)

colliding with things, they hold their antennae out in front of them in a V-shape, like obstacle detectors. If they encounter something the beetle will tip its body upwards so that it can zip right over the offending object.

EXTRAORDINARY EXOSKELETONS

Adorning our bodies with insects is something humans have done for centuries. Ever eager to catch another's eye, we decorate ourselves with the things that catch our own. The Egyptians were probably the first to wear beetles. Soldiers wore scarabs into battle, hoping to harness their supernatural powers of protection. The Victorians were rather partial to jewellery featuring tortoise beetles, and the elytra of many a pretty invertebrate has been used as earrings, necklaces or to decorate fine dresses.

We are drawn to beautiful beetles like magpies. In some cultures they pin living beetles to their chests. If you thought beetles were little brown insects bumbling around in the undergrowth, then prepare to be dazzled because I'm about to expose you to Coleoptera with the most extraordinary exoskeletons.

FROG-LEGGED LEAF BEETLE

(S a g r a   b u q u e t i) Family: Chrysomelidae

The frog-legged leaf beetle, *Sagra buqueti*, is sometimes known as the kangaroo beetle because of its gigantic hind legs. This alien-looking leaf beetle has a metallic exoskeleton, and is one of the largest and most colourful beetles on the planet. 'Leaf beetle' describes the family Chrysomelidae, which predominantly eat leaves.

Frog-legged beetles can be found in the jungles of Southeast Asia, their larvae cocooned in the soil underneath climbing vines. The first time I encountered these delightful creatures I was on an expedition to Malaysia with a research team from the University College London. I picked the beetles off vines like a child gathering sweets, finding cyan-blue ones, a cherry-red, a host of green, and some that seemed to have rainbows trapped in their exoskeletons. I laughed with delight as the miraculous frog-legged leaf beetles clambered over my hands, and for a moment I felt as if we'd all been transported to fairyland.

THIGHS OF STEEL

Despite their common name and the size of

MARVIN

The beetle has long, segmented antennae and a metallic exoskeleton rich with iridescent colour, combining to make the beetle look unreal, like a toy or a robot.

Its thorax is narrower than the base of the elytra.

FACT

Marvin is the coolest beetle in the world
v.c.w.

The giant back legs have teeth-shaped spines sticking out of them and a thick comb of orange hairs on the underside.

FIG. 28. SAGRA BUQUETI (FROG-LEGGED LEAF BEETLE)

those incredible back legs, this beetle doesn't hop or jump. It has wings, and therefore no need to jump. Instead it uses its powerful legs to climb the jungle foliage, cling on to stems and leaves while it eats, and as deadly weapons to kick, cling on to, and squeeze a rival male.

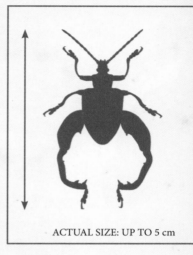

ACTUAL SIZE: UP TO 5 cm

The adult beetle eats leaves, but Hector has successfully bred frog-legged leaf beetles and he informs me <u>that they enjoy sweet potato.</u> When

Marvin loves sweet potato!

I'm standing in the middle of a rainforest, experiencing these wonderful beetles in their natural habitat, I feel a pang of sadness for my dear friend, who cannot travel abroad due to suffering from a phobia. Boats make him sick and he won't consider stepping on to an aeroplane, claiming it unnatural for humans to fly. Consequently, he will never experience the sound, smell and sight of the exotic beetles he loves so dearly in their homes. This is one of the reasons I record my expeditions thoroughly in diaries. When I return to England, I sit in Hector's glasshouse and read to him from my journal, sharing my observations and discoveries.

JEWEL BEETLE

(C h r y s o c h r o a   t o u l g o e t i)   Family: Buprestidae

I've always thought that if fairies rode steeds, they would ride the Buprestidae. They are some of the most beautiful beetles on the planet, and looking like precious stones it is no wonder they are commonly known as jewel beetles. They are a large family with some fifteen thousand species that can be found all over the globe. Different species may exhibit different colours for a number of reasons, but camouflage to avoid being eaten by predators seems to be the most likely. Insect collectors tend to prize the larger, more spectacularly coloured species.

DRESSED TO KILL

The spectacular elytra of the jewel beetle is used to make accessories, jewellery and as decoration everywhere, but particularly in Asia, India, Thailand and Japan. In Britain there is a very famous dress in Smallhythe Place in Kent that is covered in the wings of a thousand jewel beetles. It is known as the beetle wing dress and was famously worn by the actress Ellen Terry when she played Lady Macbeth in 1888. Her performance was startling, and the dress the talk of the town. So famous was it that the artist

Makes me think of Lucretia Cutter

94

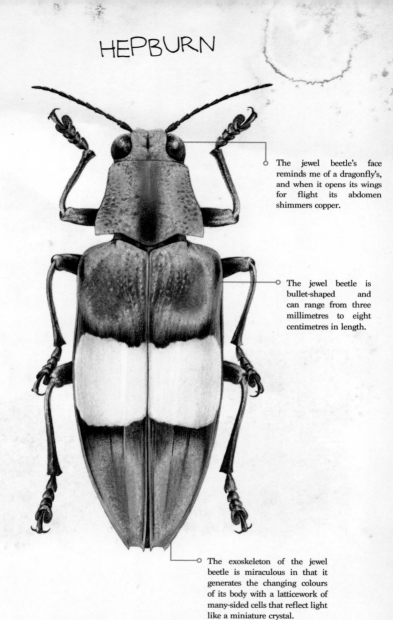

The jewel beetle's face reminds me of a dragonfly's, and when it opens its wings for flight its abdomen shimmers copper.

The jewel beetle is bullet-shaped and can range from three millimetres to eight centimetres in length.

The exoskeleton of the jewel beetle is miraculous in that it generates the changing colours of its body with a latticework of many-sided cells that reflect light like a miniature crystal.

FIG. 29. CHRYSOCHROA TOULGOETI (JEWEL BEETLE)

John Singer Sargent painted Terry wearing it, and the portrait now hangs in Tate Britain. I recommend a visit if you're ever in London, you'll get an inkling of how incredible the dress must have originally looked.

TREE DECORATIONS

The larvae of jewel beetles are known as flathead borers because they eat through roots, logs, stems and leaves of various types of plants. The female beetle lays her eggs in the cracks of tree bark, and when the larvae hatch they bore their way into the tree, feeding and growing inside the tree until they are ready to pupate and emerge as beautiful baubles. The adult beetles feed on plant foliage or nectar.

HARLEQUIN BEETLE

(Acrocinus longimanus) Family: Cerambycidae

The harlequin beetle, *Acrocinus longimanus*, is a spectacular tropical longhorn beetle native to South America. Its body can measure up to eight centimetres in length, and it feeds on sap. It gets its common name from the intricate pattern of black, red and greenish yellow markings on its wing covers, which look like the costume of the Italian theatrical comedic character

Harlequin. Its species name '*longimanus*' refers to the males' extremely long front legs, which are often longer than its entire body. The male beetle uses its ridiculously long forelegs to defend tree sap flows, a food source that will attract females. If challenged the beetle will attack other males by headbutting and biting its rivals.

The beetle may not be as funny as the cheeky character of Harlequin, but it certainly looks ridiculous. The first time I saw a harlequin beetle fly I didn't know whether to laugh or cry – so I did both.

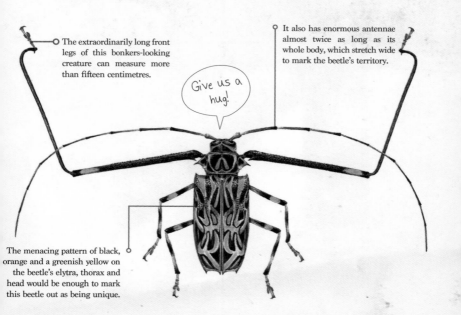

It also has enormous antennae almost twice as long as its whole body, which stretch wide to mark the beetle's territory.

The extraordinarily long front legs of this bonkers-looking creature can measure more than fifteen centimetres.

Give us a hug!

The menacing pattern of black, orange and a greenish yellow on the beetle's elytra, thorax and head would be enough to mark this beetle out as being unique.

FIG. 30. ACROCINUS LONGIMANUS (HARLEQUIN BEETLE)

FIG. 31. CYPHOCHILUS INSULANUS (SNOW WHITE BEETLE)

SNOW WHITE BEETLE

(C y p h o c h i l u s   i n s u l a n u s)   Family: Scarabaeidae

'Who is the fairest of them all?' the evil queen asked the magic mirror. Well, if by fair she meant pale, as in white, the mirror should have replied '*Cyphochilus*' for it is snow white. These beetles are famous for being the whitest example of the colour in the natural world. It achieves its perfect whiteness with a fine layer of scales that cover its exoskeleton. These scales scatter incoming light in a chaos of patterns, producing perfect white. The scarab needs to be white to camouflage itself amongst the pearly fungi found in its south-east Asian habitat. It is hiding itself from hungry birds that would gobble it up.

GOLDEN SCARAB

(Chrysina resplendens) Family: Scarabaeidae

All that glitters is not gold. Sometimes it is a beetle.

The golden scarab, *Chrysina resplendens*, when motionless, looks like a solid gold statue. These beetles are found in Panama and Costa Rica, whilst other species of *Chrysina* jewel scarabs are found in Mexico and Central America. They typically live in mountain forests, are nocturnal in their habits and are attracted to light.

The larvae live in rotting logs, eating for up to a year before pupating and emerging as golden adults. They feed on foliage and find mates up in the forest canopy, living for about three months.

GOLD ICON

As with the jewel beetle and Snow White, the golden scarab has a unique exoskeleton that manipulates light, making it appear gold. No one is certain why this beetle has a gilt exoskeleton.

The golden scarab has keen dark eyes and a pair of short-elbowed antennae.

Chrysina resplendens is typically between one-and-a-half to three-and-a-half centimetres in length.

The golden scarab is an oval beetle that looks like a perfect nugget of gold.

FIG. 32. CHRYSINA RESPLENDENS (GOLDEN SCARAB BEETLE)

It could be to blend in with its surroundings, although to my eyes it stands out. Perhaps its reflective body dazzles predators, or looks like rainwater collected in a pool upon a leaf. Alternatively, its colouration could be nothing to do with camouflage, but designed to attract a mate.

Of course, not all scarabs are a perfect gold; some look more silver or green. Nevertheless, their iridescent metallic exoskeletons are breathtaking. They send one's imagination travelling south to Ecuador, to the hunt for the Ancient Incan treasure that is lost, buried in a secret mountain cave somewhere.

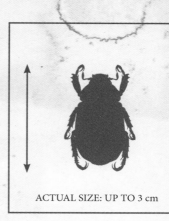

ACTUAL SIZE: UP TO 3 cm

FEATHER HORNED BEETLE

(Rhipicera femorata)   Family: Rhipiceridae

The feather horned beetle, *Rhipicera femorata*, is a mysterious, rare little thing. It is native to Australia, <u>and not much is known about the species.</u>

I had to include it in this book because the last field trip I ever took was to the wonderful wilds of Queensland, where I met a host of new beetles.

I must find out more, for Novak.

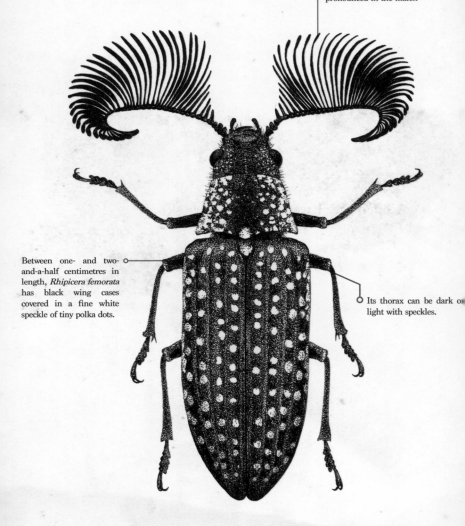

The most notable feature of both male and female feather horned beetles is the oversized fan-like antennae, which are more pronounced in the males.

Between one- and two-and-a-half centimetres in length, *Rhipicera femorata* has black wing cases covered in a fine white speckle of tiny polka dots.

Its thorax can be dark or light with speckles.

FIG. 33. RHIPICERA FEMORATA (FEATHER HORNED BEETLE)

I have to admit the feather horned beetle stole my heart away.

I had persuaded myself that a gentleman of my increasing years would look distinguished with whiskers, so I grew a beard for the visit; this was a decision I later regretted because it is rather warm in that part of the world. We were working close to Lake Awoonga when I spotted a feather horned beetle riding a stalk of grass, bobbing about in the breeze. I grabbed my sweep net, but the beetle opened its wings and escaped me. I went chasing after the thing and happened upon a field where hundreds of them were dancing about, alighting upon the grass and clinging to the trees. I looked down to grab my camera – only to see that there were two of the darling things ensnared in my beard!

I lifted them into a collection pot and sat down, deciding to draw the delightfully delicate creatures in my notebook. <u>They really are the prettiest things.</u> Their feathered antennae looked like a giant pair of eyelashes fluttering away at me. One of them had lilac downy hair underneath its abdomen and previously I had only seen the more common grey.

Perhaps a beard should be included in the list of necessary beetle-collecting equipment…

CHRISTMAS BEETLE

(Anoplognathus aureus)   Family: Scarabaeidae

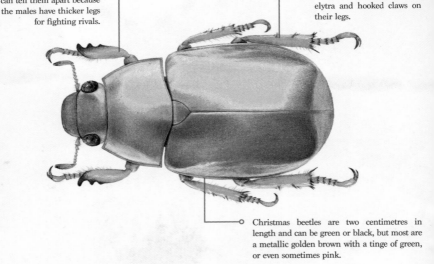

The male and female have the same colouring, but you can tell them apart because the males have thicker legs for fighting rivals.

Both sexes have an abdomen that sticks out beyond their elytra and hooked claws on their legs.

Christmas beetles are two centimetres in length and can be green or black, but most are a metallic golden brown with a tinge of green, or even sometimes pink.

FIG. 34. ANOPLOGNATHUS AUREUS (CHRISTMAS BEETLE)

Forget chestnuts roasting on an open fire and Jack Frost nipping at your nose, in Australia the festive season is heralded by the appearance of the Christmas beetle. It appears in the summer months, but in Australia that's precisely when Christmas occurs.

There are thirty-five species of metallic, golden-brown Christmas beetles. They are nocturnal, and attracted to light, so might be spotted dancing around Christmas light displays. They feed on eucalyptus leaves like the much beloved koala.

The larvae live in soil, eating decaying organic matter or plant roots. In early spring the larvae move closer to the soil surface to pupate. Adults emerge several weeks later, often after rain has softened the earth, allowing the beetles to dig their way out. They fly to the nearest eucalyptus tree to feed and mate. The females lay their eggs into soil or compost in the spring and early summer.

Christmas beetles are in decline because of urban sprawl and the increasing habitat loss of woodland areas. They have also fallen victim to drier spring weather in recent years.

~

DIABOLICAL IRONCLAD BEETLE

(Phloeodes plicatus)   Family: Zopheridae

Diabolical ironclad beetles are found worldwide and infamous for having the hardest exoskeletons of all arthropods. If you trod on this beetle and lifted your foot, it would walk away. It is said that if a motor vehicle rolled over one of these beetles it would survive. I'm uncertain where the 'diabolical' part of its common name stems from. It may be because this beetle feigns death, seemingly coming back to life after being crushed. Or perhaps its

esome!!

appearance, which is rather like a lump of hardened volcanic rock, suggests it resides in hell. This docile, flightless beetle may get its name from all the pricks, bruises and cursing it elicits from entomologists trying to pin it into a specimen drawer. It is nigh on impossible to get a pin through its tough exoskeleton; you have to drill a tiny hole first.

DRESSED UP AND PINNED DOWN

Some species look like blobs of rust or bird poo, so it is perhaps surprising that these beetles are collected to be worn as jewellery. In Mexico, ironclad beetles are decorated with costume jewels and sold as living brooches called maquech. People glue gems to the back of the beetle and attach a gold safety pin on a chain so it can walk about.

A street seller in Mexico once told me that the beetle brooch was an ancient Mayan tradition. He told me about a princess who was in love with a prince from a rival kingdom but was forbidden from marrying him. Preferring to die rather than live without him, she stopped eating and drinking. A healer with magical powers pitied the princess and transformed her from a woman to a sparkling maquech beetle. The beetle princess lived on the lapel of her lover as a beautiful brooch, over his heart.

The young chap who told me this story was enthusiastic and compelling. I have no idea whether the story was true, but no woman that I have met

FIG. 35. PHLOEODES PLICATUS (DIABOLICAL IRONCLAD BEETLE)

would be happy pinned to the collar of a man, so I bought every single one of his maquech. I took them back to my hotel room and spent the afternoon removing the jewels and chains. Taking a walk before dinner, I left the beetles on a fallen tree eating the fungus growing on the rotting wood.

Go Monty!

NOXIOUS RAPSCALLIONS

After reading my granddaughter a bedtime story, I felt the need to tell her that beetles already have the powers that people are inventing for fictional superheroes. She struggled to believe me, but was surprised and delighted when I was able to demonstrate this to be true with fireflies (flying lighthouses with vampire fangs!) and rhinoceros beetles (super-strong flying battering rams!). I suspect that all the best stories, no matter how fantastical, are inspired by observations of the real world.

YES!
YES!
YESSS!!!...

My granddaughter is a thoughtful person, and the next morning she asked me whether there were any beetles with the powers that we might give to villains. 'But of course!' I replied, and in my attempt to give her a satisfactory answer, I rounded up the noxious rapscallions. These are beetles that do some truly bizarre things that could harm you, and might scare you.

DARKLING BEETLE

(Blaps mucronata)   Family: Tenebrionidae

When asked to imagine a typical beetle, you are most likely picturing a darkling beetle. Darkling beetles are smooth and black and stereotypically 'beetle-like'. The twenty-thousand or so species of darkling beetle are common and can be found right across the globe.

The family name means 'seeker of dark places' and suggests the character of a trickster. There is a darkling beetle called the churchyard beetle, or cellar beetle, *Blaps mucronata*, that lives in old houses, hiding away in nooks and crannies during the day and coming out only at night to feed on food that has been dropped.

FIG. 36. TENEBRIONIDAE (DARKLING BEETLE)

When threatened, *Blaps mucronata* will lower its head and lift up its tail end, squirting a <u>foul-smelling chemical from the tip of its abdomen, rather like a liquid fart</u>. The fluid is an irritant, so you don't want to get it on your skin. This beetle will bite you if you annoy it. There are some darkling beetles that feign death if disturbed and then emit farts so revolting they smell like rotting corpses.

Nice!

BLISTER BEETLE

(T e g r o d e r a   a l o g a)   Family: Meloidae

Blister beetles feed on flowers and leaves and are often brightly coloured, warning predators of their toxicity. Different species of blister beetles can be found across the globe.

SUPER POWER

Blister beetles secrete a chemical called cantharidin that can cause severe blistering if it touches your skin, which is how they get their name. The cantharidin from the Spanish Fly beetle is traditionally used as a treatment for warts – and I have read was once used in love potions, which is a terrible idea, because it is poisonous! It would make people genuinely love-sick!

weird...

I've always found this cartoon of Charles Darwin riding a giant beetle rather delightful. It was drawn by his friend Albert Way when they were studying at Cambridge together and is a comment on his friend's passion for beetles.

DARWIN & his HOBBY.

Go it Charlie!

A FAMOUS STORY FROM CHARLES DARWIN ABOUT A BEETLE, WHICH HE WROTE ABOUT IN HIS AUTOBIOGRAPHY:

'... ONE DAY ON TEARING OFF SOME OLD BARK, I SAW TWO RARE BEETLES AND SEIZED ONE IN EACH HAND; THEN I SAW A THIRD AND NEW KIND, WHICH I COULD NOT BEAR TO LOSE, SO THAT I POPPED THE ONE WHICH I HELD IN MY RIGHT HAND INTO MY MOUTH. ALAS IT EJECTED SOME INTENSELY ACRID FLUID, WHICH BURNT MY TONGUE SO THAT I WAS FORCED TO SPIT THE BEETLE OUT, WHICH WAS LOST, AS WELL AS THE THIRD ONE.'

In his mouth!?
Darwin was a
DUDE!

111

Oil beetles are blister beetles that get their name from the oily droplets of chemicals that they release from their joints when disturbed.

These beetles have quite a sneaky child-rearing strategy; I think of them as the cuckoo birds of the beetle world. They dig their nest burrows in bare, tightly packed earth. The eggs hatch into larvae, which crawl up the nearest flower stem (often a celandine) and wait for a bee to come to feed. They climb on to the bee's legs and are carried back to its nest and fed by the bee, which assumes it is one of its own larvae.

Sneaky

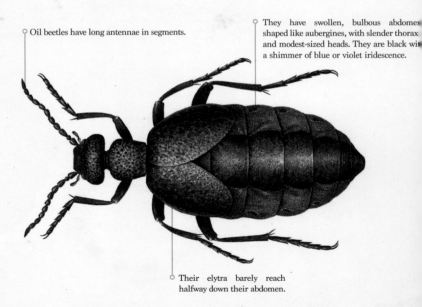

Oil beetles have long antennae in segments.

They have swollen, bulbous abdomen shaped like aubergines, with slender thorax and modest-sized heads. They are black with a shimmer of blue or violet iridescence.

Their elytra barely reach halfway down their abdomen.

FIG. 37. MELOE PROSCARABAEUS (OIL BEETLE)

BOMBARDIER BEETLE

(Brachinus   crepitans)   Family: Carabidae

Bombardier beetles are small ground beetles that don't get much bigger than a couple of centimetres in size and inhabit all continents except Antartica. Most species of bombardier beetles are carnivorous and hunt at night, feeding on other insects. Of all the superhero powers that beetles possess, this beetle has the most dangerous. I treat these beetles with a healthy respect after getting so excited upon discovering one that I got down on my belly, with my face to the ground, to collect it, and returned from my expedition empty-handed with a pox of blisters across my freshly shaven chin. Hector laughed so hard at my misfortune that I stomped out of his glasshouse and didn't dine with him for a fortnight.

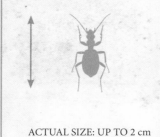

ACTUAL SIZE: UP TO 2 cm

SUPER POWER

Bombardiers are famous for their ability to shoot a boiling, toxic, chemical spray from the tip of their abdomen, like a squirt gun. It makes a popping sound when they do it and they fire with impressive

WOW!

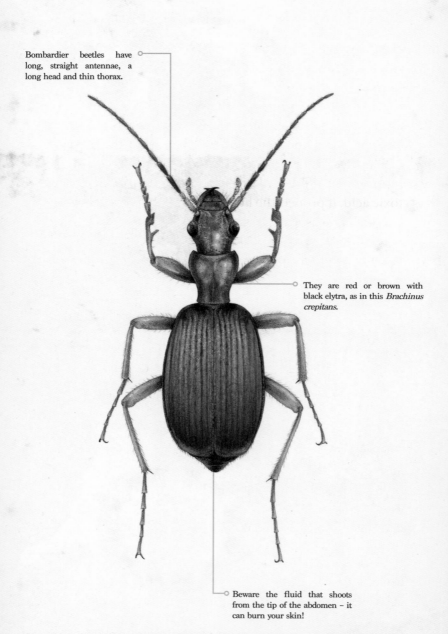

Bombardier beetles have long, straight antennae, a long head and thin thorax.

They are red or brown with black elytra, as in this *Brachinus crepitans*.

Beware the fluid that shoots from the tip of the abdomen – it can burn your skin!

FIG. 38. BRACHINUS CREPITANS (BOMBARDIER BEETLE)

accuracy. The spray can be fatal to insect predators and burn human skin – as I discovered, much to my dismay.

The beetle has different chemicals stored in two chambers in its abdomen. If it feels threatened, these two chambers flood into a third chamber at the tip of the beetle's abdomen. The resulting chemical reaction does three things: it creates a new boiling toxic acid, it propels the hot acid through the nozzle (which it points at the predator) and the power of the reaction catapults the beetle in a random direction, moving it out of harm's way.

———————— ～ ————————

DEVIL'S COACH-HORSE BEETLE

(Ocypus olens) Family: Staphylinidae

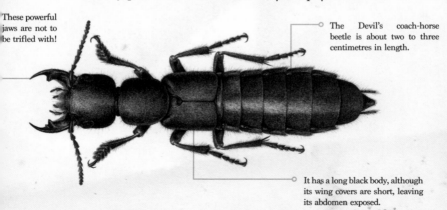

These powerful jaws are not to be trifled with!

The Devil's coach-horse beetle is about two to three centimetres in length.

It has a long black body, although its wing covers are short, leaving its abdomen exposed.

FIG. 39. OCYPUS OLENS (DEVIL'S COACH-HORSE BEETLE)

The nose biter

The Devil's coach-horse, *Ocypus olens*, is a type of rove beetle. Rove beetles are found all over the world and are the second largest family of beetles, with sixty-three thousand species. They are characterised by their short elytra and their extended, exposed abdomens. The Devil's coach-horse has stubby wing cases and is capable of flying, but rarely does. This night hunter is a predator of worms, slugs, spiders, small moths and woodlice. It nibbles its prey into a ball using its front legs and mandibles, then swallows and regurgitates it, covered in a brown digestive fluid. It keeps doing this until its prey is reduced to an edible soup. The larvae are also carnivorous, with similar disgusting eating habits.

Mmmm

The beetle is widespread in Europe and North Africa and can also be found in the Americas and Australasia. I find, in England, it is usually seen from April to October in meadows, heath and moorland, woodlands, hedgerows, parks and gardens, although during the day they hide under logs, stones or leaf litter.

SUPER POWER

The beetle has been linked to the Devil since the Middle Ages. Folklore says that the beetle ate the core of Eve's apple, and if you kill the beetle you will be forgiven seven sins. The Devil's coach-horse is well known for impersonating a scorpion when it feels threatened by lifting its abdomen and opening its jaws. Although it has no sting, the beetle can give a painful bite with its strong, pincer-like jaws, and it lets off a revolting stench from two stink glands on its abdomen.

LADYBIRD

(A n a t i s   o c e l l a t a)   Family: Coccinellidae

Are you surprised to find the ladybird here? You may not have known the ladybird was a beetle, but rest assured it is. Most people see the cheerful red-and-black, polka-dotted wing cases and smile. The ladybird is a predator of greenfly and blackfly, and other small insects, which is why gardeners and farmers love it. The 'lady' referred to in its name is the Virgin Mary. The story is that in the Middle Ages pests plagued crops, and so the farmers prayed to the Blessed Lady and miraculously these spotted beetles appeared and ate up all the pests. To humans, these beetles are a blessing.

This is a lovely story, but it doesn't give you the whole truth about our friends in the Coccinellidae. Not all ladybirds are red; there are over five thousand species all over the world and they range in colour from black through to yellow with various patterns of spots. Their bright colours relate to their species and are a warning to other creatures – predators such as birds – not to eat them.

The ladybird's dome-shaped body is a familiar figure in children's books, but rarely do we see drawings of its larvae, which look like tiny alien crocodiles, with bumpy, spiny bodies.

SUPERPOWER

Have you ever admired a ladybird on your hand only to see a yellow streak and assume that it has rather rudely gone to the toilet on you? Well, that yellow streak is not wee; it is in fact hemolymph (beetle blood), a particularly bad-tasting, smelly concoction that makes a predator spit out the beetle rather than eat it up. Ladybirds have the ability to bleed their revolting blood from their knees.

That is quite gruesome, but what is even worse is that when there are no aphids for them to eat, hungry ladybirds have been known to eat each other. WHAT?! <u>Ladybirds are cannibals!</u> They will even eat each other's babies!

Yellow ones = Lucretia Cutter's spies

FIG. 40. ANATIS OCELLATA (LADYBIRD)

AQUA SCUTTLERS

There is nothing quite as good for the body and the mind as swimming in the natural waters of rivers, lakes and seas. Whenever Hector and I plan a field trip, we always bring our bathing suits in the hope of a dip. It's good for the circulation and leaves one feeling tremendously invigorated, and, depending on where you're swimming, there's always the possibility of spotting a diving beetle. Did you know that beetles can swim? People think of beetles as land dwellers, soil diggers, wood eaters, but there are plenty of freshwater beetles that live in lakes, ponds and streams. True water beetles can be found all over the world and are very sensitive to pollution. They are a good sign of a healthy waterway. They can be found sitting just below the pond surface with their heads pointing down towards the bottom and their

We should do this.

119

tail ends sticking up out of the water. They lift the tips of their elytra to take oxygen, and when they dive they use a store of air that they trap under their wings to breathe. Not satisfied with being excellent swimmers, these beetles also fly, navigating by moonlight, looking for water by seeking its reflection.

There are over four thousand different species of diving beetles, and nearly all of them are carnivorous. So grab your pond net and dive in; it's time to meet the aqua scuttlers.

WHIRLIGIG BEETLE

(Gyrinus natator)   Family: Gyrinidae

The whirligig beetle is a versatile creature: it can be a <u>boat or a submarine, and it can fly.</u> They seek out water that flows steadily, bringing a fresh stream of food.

No way!

Apart from having a simply charming name, the whirligig beetle has two remarkable abilities. The first is the amusing habit of swimming in circles. The whirligig's family name, Gyrinidae, is Latin for circle, which is perfect because it spends much of its time paddling in circles on the surface of ponds and lakes. They don't swim in circles all of the time, or they wouldn't get anywhere; they do it when they are hunting small insects, if they feel threatened, and also as a water dance to impress female whirligigs. The second impressive feature of these beetles is that they have divided eyes, and can see both above and below the water.

The whirligig lays its eggs underwater on water plants in rows, and the larvae are vicious little beasties with jaws like needles; they consume their prey rather like fireflies by turning them into soup. In the autumn,

FIG. 41. GYRINIDAE (WHIRLIGIG BEETLE)

the adults fly off in search of another waterhole.

SYNCHRONISED SWIMMING

You will find whirligig beetles in groups, moving in what looks like a chaotic pattern. However, each whirligig has a specific place in the group and they communicate continuously with one another. Unlike other water animals such as fish or sea lions, beetles have unbending exoskeletons. They are like tiny boats with some of their body above the water and some below. They spin in tight circles using their legs or wings for propulsion, and if frightened they will dive underwater, using an air bubble attached to the tip of their abdomen to enable them to stay under for long periods.

GREAT DIVING BEETLE

(D y t i s c u s   m a r g i n a l i s)   Family: Dytiscidae

The great diving beetle is one of the biggest aquatic beetles in the world. It can be found in Europe and northern Asia and is a common sight in waters near my home in Britain. This fierce predator will feast on whatever it can catch, including small frogs and not-so-small fish. Although it can fly – and will do so if it needs to find new watery hunting ground – the great diving beetle spends much of its time underwater.

In some countries eating water beetle flesh is a delicacy, and I'm told it tastes like crab meat. *Hmmmm, no thanks!*

BREATHING UNDERWATER

To keep from drowning, the beetles have tiny hairs on their abdomens that keep water away from their spiracles. When this bristly beetle dives, a thin, silvery layer of air is carried with it, and the beetle uses this to breathe underwater.

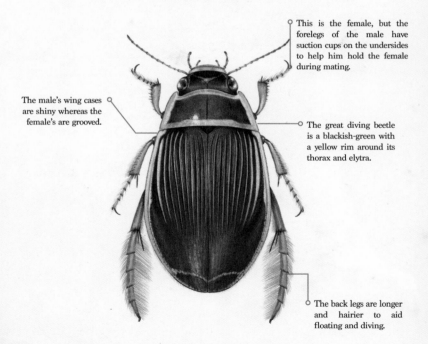

This is the female, but the forelegs of the male have suction cups on the undersides to help him hold the female during mating.

The male's wing cases are shiny whereas the female's are grooved.

The great diving beetle is a blackish-green with a yellow rim around its thorax and elytra.

The back legs are longer and hairier to aid floating and diving.

FIG. 42. DYTISCUS MARGINALIS (GREAT DIVING BEETLE)

SCAT SQUAD

Do you like dung? No, of course not. Well, if it wasn't for the many species of dung beetle busily breaking down animal droppings every day, you'd be wading to school in wellington boots through an ocean of the stinky stuff. We humans might not like poo, but in the natural world dung is a precious resource rich with nutrients.

'Dung beetle' is a common name for any beetle that feeds partly or entirely on poo. There are three types of dung beetle: the rollers, the tunnellers and the dwellers. The dwellers live in the dung, whereas the other two bury it. Dung beetles are extremely useful recyclers and can be found on every continent in the world except Antarctica.

SACRED SCARAB

(S c a r a b a e u s   s a c e r)   Family: Scarabaeidae

SCUD

The sacred scarab has a head plate with a jagged edge; this echoes the protrusions on its short front legs. These sticky-out bumps, which are said to resemble the rays of the sun, are used for digging and shaping dung balls.

The front legs of this scarab seem too short, as if missing a bit. The mid and hind leg are of a normal length.

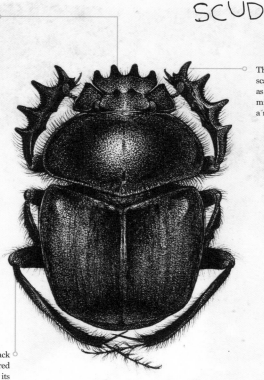

The beetle is usually black or brown with rust-coloured hairs protruding from its joints and can be up to three centimetres in length.

FIG. 43. SCARABAEUS SACER (SACRED SCARAB BEETLE)

The sacred scarab, *Scarabaeus sacer*, is the most famous of all scarab beetles because the Ancient Egyptians used it as a symbol for Khepri, the god of the rising sun. The Egyptians saw the beetle's behaviour, of rolling a dung ball across the sand, as a mirror of Khepri's daily task: rolling the sun across the sky. The symbol of the scarab is a common hieroglyph found in tombs. It conveys ideas of transformation, renewal and resurrection. Heart scarabs, made from green stone and placed over the heart of the dead, were supposed to ensure the heart would not reveal all of the dead person's guilty secrets when they came to be judged in the afterlife. Images of the sacred scarab can be found in many Egyptian carvings and paintings, or on jewellery.

BALL BEARINGS

The behaviour of the sacred scarab is typical of rollers. It collects dung into balls, walks backwards on its front legs – in a handstand – and rolls the ball with its hind legs to a safe location. There it digs an underground chamber in which to hide the ball. When the female is ready, she will build a breeding ball out of fine-textured dung and dig an especially deep hole for it. She moulds it into a pear shape, making a hole in the narrow bit into which she lays a single egg. She then covers up the hole, and, when the egg hatches, the larva feeds on the dung. A female beetle will typically produce only about six eggs in her lifetime.

OLD AS TIME

Dung beetles were on this planet long before us, and there will probably be dung beetles labouring away in the muck after we humans have gone. We know dung beetles were trundling the earth thirty million years ago, and that they were giants in comparison to beetles living today. How do we know this? It's because grapefruit-sized, fossilised dung balls have been found by palaeontologists, who think the balls were made from the dung of armadillos as large as a motor vehicle!

GIANT BEETLES!

STAR NAVIGATOR

The dung beetle is the first insect shown to be able to navigate by the stars. You see, dung beetles roll their balls in a straight line, which is not easy when you are pushing it from behind, standing upside down, with your face to the ground. Before it rolls a ball, the dung beetle will climb on top of it to get its bearings. Scientific experiments had already shown that the beetles are able to steer by light from the sun and the moon, but it was their ability to stay on course on clear, moonless nights that puzzled researchers.

Then a scientist called Dr Marie Dacke performed a series of experiments with *Scarabaeus satyrus*, beetles similar to the sacred scarab and can be found in South Africa and Namibia. She brought the beetles inside a planetarium in Johannesberg, South Africa, where she could control the night sky. When Dr Dacke placed tiny hats on them, blocking out the night sky, they wandered about aimlessly. But when they were able to see the Milky Way, they could steer their ball straight home.

MINOTAUR BEETLE

(Typhaeus typhoeus)   Family: Geotrupidae

One of the most impressive-looking of European dung beetles is *Typhaeus typhoeus*, the Minotaur beetle. It is a large, round dung beetle that can be found in sandy grassland and heathland. Its family name, Geotrupidae, means 'earth-borer', and it accordingly tunnels below piles of rabbit or sheep droppings, making burrows, which can be easily provisioned with poop. Their nest tunnels can reach a metre-and-a-half in depth and are labyrinthine. Adults emerge in autumn, but aren't ready to breed until they've gone through a phase of eating. Once they have eaten their fill, they lay their eggs in their burrows, providing dung for the larvae to feed on. Minotaur larvae stay safe underground,

FIG. 44. TYPHAEUS TYPHOEUS (MINOTAUR BEETLE)

feasting on herbivore dung meals in side branches of the tunnels, built and stocked by their parents.

If you are going Minotaur hunting, find piles of sheep or rabbit droppings and search for tunnel entrances, which are about one centimetre in diameter. The adults overwinter as pairs in the burrow and will emerge on mild winter days. Once they have eaten their fill, the larvae pupate and the new generation of adult beetles generally emerge in the autumn. I was once discovered by a pair of hikers, as I peered into a burrow on all fours with my nose to the ground. It looked to them as if I was sniffing the sheep droppings, and my hastily muttered explanation about the Minotaur beetle was met with disbelieving stares. I didn't mind, though, because not fifteen minutes later I spotted a male and spent a delightful afternoon sketching him.

CARING COLEOPTERA

Dung beetles are nurturing creatures. The mummy beetle will build an underground nest and stuff it with provisions of poop for her children. She deposits each individual egg in its own tiny dung sausage so that when the larvae emerge, they are well-supplied with food. There are some species within, *Copris* and *Ontophagus*, in which both parents share the childcare duties, and there are some *Cephalodesmius* dung beetles that mate for life. I admit I feel affectionately towards the beetle, purely for its exemplary parenting practices, because I was packed off to boarding school at the age of five, and whilst it was a character-building education, I rather hanker after a nurturing family and have attempted to emulate the dung beetle when bringing up my own children.

TAURUS BEETLE
(Onthophagus taurus) Family: Scarabaeidae

The Taurus scarab, *Onthophagus taurus*, is an efficient recycler and, although it comes from the Mediterranean, it has been exported around the world to deal with dung.

FIG. 45. ONTHOPHAGUS TAURUS (TAURUS BEETLE)

WORLD'S STRONGEST ANIMAL

Onthophagus taurus is the world's strongest animal, relative to its size. This is because it can pull over a thousand times its own weight, which is like a human pulling eighty tons or dragging six fully-laden double-decker buses!

So is the dung beetle stronger than Baxter?

Even a small ball of fresh dung can be difficult to push, weighing fifty times what the determined dung beetle does. The boys have to be strong, not just for the pushing and pulling of poo balls, but for the fisticuffs with other males hoping to muscle in on their mate. The girls dig

131

the tunnels under dung pats, and the boys come looking for them. If a male beetle goes into a tunnel that is already occupied, they lock horns and fight, trying to push each other out.

POWER TEST

The Taurus scarab's claim to fame is based on a different assessment of strength to a rhinoceros beetle being able to lift eight-hundred-and-fifty times its own weight – see page 43. And in this instance, Dr Rob Knell of Queen Mary, University of London, and Professor Leigh Simmons from the University of Western Australia have shown the Taurus scarab can pull 1,141 times its own body weight. They placed a beetle in an artificial tunnel, with a string glued to its back. The string fed out of the tunnel and over a pulley, where it was attached to a pot. During the experiment, water was slowly dripped into the pot, which pulled on the string, until the beetle could no longer resist being pulled backwards. A simple calculation was then made about the weight of water in the pot in relation to the weight of the beetle.

SMALL DUNG BEETLE

(A p h o d i i n a e)   Family: Scarabaeidae

The small dung beetle is from a subfamily of the scarab beetle called *Aphodiinae*. They are generally dung dwellers and so most do not roll or burrow, but simply live in manure. They are small with long bodies that are black or brown in colour. The females lay eggs in fresh dung, and when the larvae hatch they happily munch away on the poo that surrounds them.

FIG. 46. APHODIINAE (SMALL DUNG BEETLE)

Most dung beetles can fly, and must, quickly, to get to fresh manure first. I have been on field trips to Africa where I've counted nearly four thousand dung beetles on a fresh pile of elephant scat a mere fifteen minutes after it hit the ground. Within the hour there were in excess of ten thousand, too many to count. I can guess that you are reading this thinking, *Really, did you sit for an hour counting beetles arriving on fresh poo?* And of course the answer is: yes! It was marvellous fun to see the beetles merrily rolling their balls away. This is one of the great joys of being an entomologist.

AWESO
I want
do this

FARMER'S FRIEND

Dung beetles are a farmer's friend. They work tirelessly clearing fields of manure that might otherwise attract bloodsucking animal pests. By dragging dung into the ground they fertilise and enrich the soil and tunnellers create drainage and irrigate the land. A clever farmer will do all they can to encourage dung beetles on to their farm, because one cow can produce over nine tonnes of dung in a year.

However, our dung beetles are disappearing because of the medicines we use to treat cattle. These come out in the dung, and they can poison the beetles.

Pestici
are BA

BLOOMING BEETLES

Most people know that bees are important pollinators and that we must protect and encourage them. However, very few people realise that there are more plants on this planet pollinated by beetles than bees. One of the simplest ways of finding beetles is to go out walking through a meadow of wildflowers with a sweep net. As you work your way through the grass, you'll catch many beetle flower fanciers in your net. Some beetles greedily eat up plants at such a voracious rate that they are considered pests. Some beetles are essential to the flower's pollination. Sometimes a beetle can have an impact on plants that elevates them to the astonishing status of biological weapon. Make way, for here come the blooming beetles!

COLORADO POTATO BEETLE

(Leptinotarsa decemlineata)   Family: Chrysomelidae

With its yellow-and-black striped elytra, the Colorado potato beetle looks like a tiny, rotund member of a barbershop quartet; all he needs is a little straw hat! However, in the First and Second World Wars this beetle was considered a deadly weapon. This is because *Leptinotarsa decemlineata* is a serious pest to potato crops.

Native to the United States of America and Mexico, this hungry beetle can now be found throughout Europe and Asia.

WEAPON OF SPUD DESTRUCTION

In 1950, after the Second World War, the East German government claimed the Americans were dropping potato beetle bombs out of their planes on to fields to sabotage their crops. Politicians called the beetles the 'six-legged ambassadors of the American invasion'!

Leaflets and posters were produced depicting the potato beetles as tiny American soldiers, and the Colorado potato beetle was nicknamed the Yankee beetle. After school, children would be sent out to pick beetles and their larvae off potato plants. A single potato-munching beetle can lay eight hundred eggs and is resistant to insecticides, so an infestation

136

FIG. 47. LEPTINOTARSA DECEMLINEATA (COLORADO POTATO BEETLE)

could destroy a crop that most people depended on for food.

The truth is not as exciting as the stories told by the East German government. The anti-American propaganda campaign was a way of getting the people to unite and battle the beetle; the Colorado potato beetle was already a problem in Germany before the Second World War.

BLUE MONKEY BEETLE

(Scelophysa trimeni)   Family: Scarabaeidae

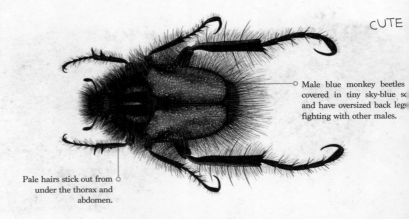

CUTE

Male blue monkey beetles [are] covered in tiny sky-blue s[cales] and have oversized back leg[s for] fighting with other males.

Pale hairs stick out from under the thorax and abdomen.

FIG. 48. SCELOPHYSA TRIMENI (BLUE MONKEY BEETLE)

The blue monkey beetle, *Scelophysa trimeni*, is a delightful small scarab beetle found in South Africa. The nights in South Africa can get extremely cold, a fact I learned first-hand when sleeping in a tent on expedition. To keep warm, I ended up putting on all the clothes I'd brought with me before getting into my bed, which almost ruined my three-piece suit. To protect itself from the cold, the monkey beetle will spend the night within the closed petals of a daisy. This not only keeps it warm, but also covers it in pollen. When the sun rises and the flower opens, the male blue monkey beetle flies off in search of a mate, hopping from flower to flower, pollinating and feeding off the nectar as he goes.

TANSY BEETLE

(Chrysolina graminis)   Family: Chrysomelidae

A beautifully iridescent green beetle that flickers with gold and red as it shimmers in the sun. The Victorians so admired the wings of the Tansy that they used the elytra as sequins to decorate clothes. This adorably bumbling creature gets its name from the plant on which it is dependent. If you are extremely lucky and somewhere beside the river Ouse, near the city of York in England, in the months of April, May or June, you may spot the

I've never seen a Tansy beetle.

FIG. 49. CHRYSOLINA GRAMINIS (TANSY BEETLE)

iridescent elytra of this fair fellow.

The beetle's eggs look like yellow grains of saffron rice and can be found on the underside of tansy leaves. The larvae are the ugly duckling to the adult beetle's swan, with a bulbous beige body and a brown head. They hatch between May and July into larvae, which feed hungrily on the leaves. When they've eaten their fill, they burrow in to the ground at the base of the plant and make themselves an earth cocoon in which they become a pupa. In August the new adults emerge and can be spotted on the yellow button tansy flowers. At the end of the summer they overwinter underground, returning in April, when they feed, mate and lay eggs.

Once upon a time the tansy beetle could be found across the wetlands of Britain, but sadly it is now endangered in my home and across its worldwide range. The beetles can fly but only for very short distances, and don't seem to like to. As tansy is their sole food source, if a thicket of tansy disappears, the beetles have to walk till they find a new one.

MAY BUG

(Melonlontha melolontha) Family: Scarabaeidae

The May bug, or chafer, can be found throughout Europe, and a similar species found in North America is known as the June bug. The large white larvae of these beetles feed on the roots of grasses and are the enemy of cricket-lawn tenders and bowling-green managers. The damage is worsened by crows and foxes, who will dig up turf in search of the tasty grub.

The beetles come out of the ground in late spring, seemingly from nowhere, and form swarms, usually on low trees and shrubs. They are most active on warm clear nights, returning to the soil at daybreak.

These beetles have one-year life cycles, but the adult beetles only live for two weeks. The female chafers will lay up to forty eggs in the ground, which take two weeks to hatch. The lawn-munching larvae are white with an ochre yellow head and tend to be C-shaped and the size of trouser buttons. They will feed until frosts fall, when they will burrow deeper. As spring warms the soil, they feed more vigorously, and in June the grubs move deeper into the soil, build earthen cocoons and pupate inside over two weeks, until the adult beetles start emerging.

FIG. 50. MELONLONTHA MELOLONTHA (MAY BUG)

AN ENTOMOLOGIST'S EPILOGUE

E very creature in the earth's ecosystem has a role to play in the healthy functioning of this planet. It is frightening to think about what might happen if we lose a significant number of creatures in years to come. While we may not notice if a species of beetle becomes extinct, the role it performed – whether that be as a food source for small mammals and birds, pollinating flowers, or cleaning up dung – will go unfilled. We cannot know what impact that will have.

This uncertain future is not what troubles me most about the number of beetles that are under threat, endangered or have already become extinct.

What troubles me is that the cause of much of this loss is us, the human race.

I want to enlist your help, to save and preserve the beetles that are endangered. I'm asking you to become a guardian of the wild, a protector of nature. Go out and hunt for beetles, find their habitats, record them and protect them. Take your friends and family and teach them the way of the beetle. Together we can all make a difference. You may not be able to fight to save a faraway rainforest, but you can help to protect a native species of beetle that comes from the same part of the world as you. *YES!*

So from Hector, who has no children but very much approves of my writing this book, and myself, hear our war cry: 'Go outside! Get muddy! Swim in lakes! Dig about in droppings (making sure to wash your hands afterwards) and rummage in the undergrowth!' For there is no greater adventure than meeting the creatures we share this planet with.

As my hero, and the godfather of entomology, Jean Henri Fabre once wrote:

'WHAT MATTERS IN LEARNING IS NOT TO BE TAUGHT, BUT TO WAKE UP.'

I AM AWAKE!!!

M.G. LEONARD

IT'S OK TO BE
SCARED OF INSECTS

I didn't always love beetles. When I was a girl I was frightened of creepy crawlies. Not the fun kind of thrilling fear, but the running-away-screaming kind of fear. That fear didn't go away when I grew up.

When I started writing *Beetle Boy*, the insects weren't the good guys, but I wanted to describe them well. I looked up beetles on the Internet. I read the facts, looked at pictures and was astonished to learn how important beetles are to the planet. I had no idea how many different kinds of beetles there were in the world and I was struck by their beauty. As I discovered the truth about beetles, I realised this world is a wonderland of insects. I'd been too busy running away from bugs to actually look at them properly. I tore out beetle articles from magazines and newspapers. I bought DVDs and spent hours listening to David Attenborough telling me all about *Micro Monsters* and *Life in the Undergrowth*. I started to notice beetles in my own garden. I didn't realise it, but my fear was being replaced by something else: fascination.

When the first draft of *Beetle Boy* was written, my growing passion for beetles had changed the story. The beetles are the heroes of the book, the good guys, like they are in nature. I wanted to make their skills integral to the plot.

I cared deeply about getting the facts in the book correct. I wanted to use the right words to describe them. I searched for an entomologist who could help me. This is how I met Dr Sarah Beynon. I saw her on TV, on a programme called *Countryfile*, talking about her bug farm. I wrote her an email explaining that I'd written a book and wanted the beetles in the story to be accurately represented. She became the scientific consultant for my trilogy and has taught me so much. A year after our first correspondence, I visited Sarah's bug farm and met Robert the rainbow stag beetle. Sarah helped me to pick up and hold a beetle for the first time, and as he happily crawled up my arm I felt proud and amazed. My fear had vanished; I fell in love with Robert and immediately wanted my own rainbow stag beetle. Six weeks later I had a terrarium in my study with a pair of them, Hector and Motticilla.

Welcoming these six-legged wonders into my head, my heart and my home has brought me more joy, knowledge and inspiration than any other single pursuit in my life. Beetles have changed me for the better, and I hope they will forgive me for having squealed and run away from them for thirty years. I plan to make up for it by writing books that will enable readers to understand beetles better. I want to fill the planet with Beetle Girls and Beetle Boys who love all of the natural world, but especially the invertebrates.

DR SARAH BEYNON

LIFE ON THE BUG FARM

I've been fascinated by insects for as long as I remember. Gran, Mum and I would go on adventures around our farm looking for the amazing hidden life in the undergrowth, gently grabbing whatever beetle moved, or trapping it in a home-made pitfall trap. We would then pop it in a bug box so we could take it home to study. Back home, we would first watch and record the beetle's behaviour before using an encyclopaedia to learn more about it. After learning about it, we would draw up a food web, linking the beetle to what it ate and what ate it, and then draw it before releasing it back where we caught it.

LIFE AS AN ENTOMOLOGIST

Being an entomologist is THE best job if you want to have adventures. I have gone beetle-hunting in the Amazon Rainforest and, in the mountains of Honduras, I have lured in the most colourful, rare and exotic beetles using giant light traps. I have explored the cloud forests of Ecuador, investigated the lush valleys nestled between red table mountains in Bolivia and trekked deep into areas of Atlantic rainforest in Brazil that haven't been entered by humans for over fifty years. I have tracked dung beetles with tiny radio transmitters in Zambia and have even found a new species of beetle in an old, discarded plastic cup!

Each expedition comes with danger. Whilst monitoring dung beetles in Honduras, I stepped on a fer-de-lance snake – one of the most poisonous snakes in the world. It chased me for a hundred metres before, luckily, I fell, unbitten, off the side of a mountain. Unfortunately, I fell quite a long way and landed in a prickly tree; I spent the next week nursing my bruises and removing thorns from my bottom. Then there was the time my tent was trampled by a herd of elephants ... when I was still in it. Expeditions are exciting, and I can't wait for the next one.

If you find yourself in the Pembrokeshire Coast National Park, be sure to come and visit us at the Bug Farm, a 100-acre working farm, research centre and visitor attraction all about invertebrates ('bugs'). We have the best team here to help you delve into the wonders of life in the undergrowth. In our Tropical Bug Zoo you will meet some of the world's largest and most colourful invertebrates: we have a prehistoric giant vinegaroon, who shoots vinegar out of her backside; a leafcutter ant colony; Rosie, my pet tarantula; and giant metallic flower beetles chomping on beetle jelly. You can meet Steve the giant thorny stick insect, Jeff the giant Madgascan hissing cockroach, and let Jessica the green bean stick insect climb on to your head! Or put on your wellies and have a stomp around outside; you may capture a bloody-nosed beetle or even net *Araneus quadratus* – the heaviest spider in the UK!

Sarah Beynon

Sarah Beynon owns Dr Beynon's Bug Farm. She is a Senior Research Associate of the University of Oxford and a Fellow of the Royal Entomological Society.

MAX BARCLAY

AFTERWORD

According to my mother, I was picking up insects since before I could talk. Specimens I found as a boy are now in the national collections. I will always remember finding my first stag beetle, my first wasp beetle, and, much later, my first new species.

I have been on several expeditions with the Natural History Museum to South and Central America and South-East Asia, to tropical rainforests and mountain cloud forests, where the insect life is most diverse. My colleagues and I have discovered several hundred new species, amazing insects never seen before, and I have had the opportunity to name a few of them. You don't need to travel the world, though, to collect and study insects, or even to make new discoveries. There are things to discover on our own doorsteps.

The Natural History Museum collection is one of the most important archives of biodiversity in the world. It collects the knowledge of the centuries – the fruits of thousands of expeditions concentrated together in one place, and it is consulted by hundreds of scientists and students from all over the world every year. We have 22,000 drawers of beetles, more than 10 million specimens. It is one of the greatest treasure-troves in the world, and from the time I first saw it as a teenager I knew it was where I wanted to spend the rest of my life. Every specimen in a collection has labels saying where it was from, who collected it, what it is; collections are like the great libraries of ancient times, they are a storehouse of all of human knowledge about the natural world, all in one place.

Many people, especially many adults, think insects are either scary or not very interesting. Those attitudes are so incredibly short-sighted, and people miss out by not having their eyes open to the wonders all around them. The world needs beetles, and people need books like *Beetle Boy* to remind everyone how important insects are.

There's a famous saying from a Senegalese conservationist Baba Dioum, that we only conserve what we love, and we only love what we know about, and we only know about what we're taught. Knowledge is the key to conservation, and the more people know about insects and the natural habitats that support them, the more people will want to preserve them. With many of the world's most wonderful environments under threat, at home and abroad, it has never been more urgent for people, especially young people, to know and care about insects and nature. As this book shows, the world all around us is full of amazing things to see, learn and discover.

Max V. L. Barclay

Max Barclay is a leading world expert on insects, and the Curator of Beetles at the Natural History Museum in London.

AN ENTOMOLOGIST'S DICTIONARY

ABDOMEN	In humans, the abdomen is called the tummy or belly. In insects the abdomen is the bit of the body behind the thorax. It is the largest of the three body segments of an insect (the other parts being the head and the thorax).
ANTENNAE	A pair of sensory appendages on the head sometimes called 'feelers'. They are used to sense many things including odour, taste, heat, wind speed and direction. (Singular = antenna.)
ARTHROPOD	Arthropod means 'jointed leg' and refers to a group of animals that includes the insects (known as hexapods), crustaceans, myriapods (millipedes and centipedes) and chelicerates (spiders, scorpions, horseshoe crabs and their relatives). Arthropod bodies are usually in segments and all arthropods have exoskeletons – skeletons on the outside of their bodies rather than on the inside like us. All arthropods are invertebrates.
BEETLE	Beetles are one type (or 'Order') of insect with the front pair of wings hardened into wing cases (elytra). There are more different species of beetle than any other animal on the planet.
CHITIN	Chitin is one of the most important substances in nature. It is the material that makes up the exoskeletons of most arthropods, including the insects.
COLEOPTERA	The scientific name for beetles.
COLEOPTERIST	A scientist who studies beetles.

COMPOUND EYE	Common in arthropods, compound eyes can be made up of thousands of individual visual receptors. They enable many arthropods to see very well, but they see the world as a pixelated image – like the pixels on a computer screen.
DNA	DNA (deoxyribonucleic acid) is the blueprint for almost every living creature. It is the molecule that carries genetic information. A length of DNA is called a gene. DNA molecules are tightly packed around proteins to make chromosomes. A chromosome can contain hundreds or thousands of genes.
DOUBLE HELIX	The shape which DNA forms when the individual components of DNA join together. It looks like a twisted ladder.
ELYTRA	The elytra (singular = elytron) are the hardened forewings of beetles and serve as protective wing-cases for the delicate, membranous hindwings underneath, which are used for flying. Some beetles can't fly; their elytra are fused together and they don't have hindwings.
ENTOMOLOGIST	A scientist who studies insects.
EXOSKELETON	An external skeleton. Insects have exoskeletons made largely from chitin. The exoskeleton is very strong and can be jam-packed with muscles, meaning that insects (especially beetles which have extremely tough exoskeletons) can be very strong for their size.
HABITAT	The area in which an organism lives. This is not the specific location. For example, a stag beetle's habitat is a broad-leaved woodland and not London.
INSECT	Insects are in the 'Class' Insecta, with over 1.8 million different species known and more to discover. Insects have three main body parts, the head, thorax and abdomen. The head has antennae and a pair of compound eyes. Insects have six legs and many have wings. Many have a complex lifecycle called metamorphosis.

INVERTEBRATE	An invertebrate is an animal that does not have a spine (backbone).
LARVAE	Larvae (singular = larva) are immature insects. Beetle larvae are often called grubs. Larvae look completely different to adult beetles and often feed on different things than their parents, meaning that they don't compete with their parents for food.
MANDIBLES	Mandibles are the beetles' mouthparts. Mandibles can grasp, crush or cut food, or defend against predators and rivals.
METAMORPHOSIS	Metamorphosis means 'change'. It involves a total transformation of the insect between the different life stages (egg, larvae, pupae and adult or egg, nymphs, adult). For example, imagine a big, fat, cream grub: it looks nothing like an adult beetle. Many insects (including beetles) metamorphosise inside pupae or cocoons: they enter the pupae as grubs, are dissolved into beetle soup, re-form as adult beetles and break their way out of the pupae. Adult beetles never moult and, as they are encased in a hard exoskeleton that doesn't stretch or grow, they can never grow bigger. Therefore, if you see an adult beetle, it can never grow any bigger than it is.
PALPS	A pair of sensory appendages near the mouth of an insect. They are used to touch/feel and sense chemicals in the surroundings.
SETAE	Tiny hair-like projections covering parts of an insect's body. They may be protective, can be used for defence, camouflage and adhesion (sticking to things) and can be sensitive to moisture and vibration. (singular = seta.)
SPECIES	See 'Taxonomy'. The species is the scientific name for an organism and helps us define what type of organism something is, irrespective of what language you speak. For example, across the world, Baxter will be known as *Chalcosoma caucasus*. However, depending what language you speak, you will call him a different common name. The species name is a written with its genus name in front of it and it is typed in italics, with the genus starting with a capital letter and the species all in lower-case type.

STRIDULATION	A loud squeaking or scratching noise made by an insect rubbing its body parts together, to attract a mate, as a territorial sound or warning sign.
TAXONOMY	The practice of identifying, describing and naming organisms. It uses a system called 'biological classification', with similar organisms grouped together. It starts off with a broad grouping (the kingdom) and gets more specific, with the species as the most specific group. No two species names (when combined with their genus) are the same: kingdom → phylum → class → order → family → genus → species. This system avoids the confusion caused by common names, which vary in different languages or even different households. For example, Baxter is a species of rhinoceros beetle: some people may call him an atlas beetle, Hercules beetle or unicorn beetle, and there are lots of different species of rhinoceros beetle. So how do we know what Baxter really is? If you use biological classification, you can classify Baxter as: kingdom = Animalia (animal) → phylum = Arthropoda (arthropod) → class = insecta (insect) → order = Coleoptera → family = Scarabaeidae → genus = *Chalcosoma* → species = *caucasus*. But all you really need to say is the genus and species, so Baxter is: *Chalcosoma caucasus*.
THORAX	The part of an insect's body between the head and the abdomen.
TRANSGENIC	An animal can be described as transgenic if scientists have added DNA from another species.

STANDING ON THE SHOULDERS OF GIANTS

I have tried to be thorough when doing the research for this book. Nevertheless, our understanding of the natural world grows and changes with time. I've asked entomologists to proof this text so it is worthy of the children who will read it. I am not an entomologist. I am a children's writer, and describe myself as a beetle tourist or enthusiast. Before I set out to write about beetles I knew very little about the creatures with which I am now enamoured. I am well aware that to produce a book like this I am standing on the shoulders of giants. I would like to acknowledge all of the entomologists around the world that do the hard research that is then reduced into facts for consumption by an enthusiast like me. I have absorbed information from a wealth of places, but I must acknowledge the following:

Brilliant Beetle Books: An Inordinate Fondness for Beetles by Arthur V. Evans and Charles L. Bellamy, *The Book of Beetles* edited by Patrice Bouchard, *A Coleopterist's Handbook*, edited by J. Cooter and M.V.L. Barclay, *British Insects* by George E. Hyde, *Life on Earth* by David Attenborough, *The Young Beetle Collector's Handbook* by E. Hofmann, *The Sacred Beetle and Others, The Life of the Weevil,* and *The Glow-Worm and Other Beetles* by Jean Henri Fabre.

WONDERFUL WEBSITES:

www.nationalgeographic.com
www.buglife.org.uk
www.ptes.org.uk
www.thoughtCo.com
www.bbc.co.uk
www.arkive.org
www.insectidentification.org
www.wildlifetrusts.org

www.amentsoc.org
www.royensoc.co.uk
www.sciencenews.org
www.livescience.com
www.featuredcreature.com
www.bugguide.net
www.drbeynonsbugfarm.com
www.nhm.ac.uk

These are all great places to go and continue discovering more about the weird and wild world of invertebrates.

ACKNOWLEDGEMENTS

I would like to thank the passionate entomologists around the world for their wonderful work, and in particular, Sarah Beynon, Max Barclay, Jess French, Simon Leather, Christopher Jeffs and Ashleigh Whiffin. A big thank you to the amazing team at Scholastic, especially Linas Alsenas, Liam Drane and Miriam Farbey, who've worked so hard to make this book everything I dreamed it could be. Special thanks and buckets of gratitude go to artist Carim Nahaboo whose illustrations elevate this book, making it a thing of beauty. Thanks to my agent Kirsty McLachlan and publisher Barry Cunningham for creating the opportunity for this book to exist, and last but not least, to my husband Sam Sparling, without whom I could not be an author.

PHOTO CREDITS